The Paul Mace Guide to Data Recovery

Paul Mace

Brady
New York

BRADY

Simon & Schuster, Inc.
Gulf + Western Building
One Gulf + Western Plaza
New York, NY 10023

Distributed by Prentice Hall Trade

Manufactured in the United States of America

10 9 8 7 6 5 4 3 2 1

Library of Congress Cataloging-in-Publication Data
Mace, Paul.
[Guide to data recovery]
  The Paul Mace guide to data recovery / Paul Mace.
    p.   cm.

Includes index.
    1. Data recovery (Computer science)   I. Title
II. Title: Guide to data recovery.
QA76.9.D348M33   1988
005.7—dc19   88-29765 CIP
ISBN 0-13-654427-4

64990

Limits of Liability and Disclaimer of Warranty

The author and publisher of this book have used their best efforts in preparing this book and the programs contained in it. These efforts include the development, research, and testing of the theories and programs to determine their effectiveness. The author and publisher make no warranty of any kind, expressed or implied, with regard to these programs or the documentation contained in this book. The author and publisher shall not be liable in any event for incidental or consequential damages in connection with or arising out of, the furnishing, performance, or use of these programs.

Trademarks

Dedication

For Kathleen, who never trusts a computer.

Epigraph

"We become authorities and experts in the practical and scientific spheres by so many separate acts and hours of work. If anyone keeps faithfully busy each hour of the working day, he may safely leave the final result to itself. He can with perfect certainty count on waking up some fine morning to find himself one of the competent ones of his generation . . . silently, between all the details of his business, the 'power of judging' . . . will have built itself up within him."

—William James

Contents

Introduction

Discovery often begins in carelessness. If Fleming had thought to close the laboratory window, we wouldn't have penicillin. If I hadn't been in a hurry four years ago, DOS Format would still be considered a lethal operation.

I was working on a hard disk defragger, from curiosity. (I was supposed to be working on a novel, but like many others, word-processing had led to liking computers, liking had led to loving, and loving had led to more intimate involvement.) The project was going slowly. I had to back everything up after every change, as testing meant, more often than not, clobbering the disk in new and exciting ways. Afterward I'd inspect the damage with Debug, then reformat and restore the backups.

In the middle of my fourth or fifth Format I realized I hadn't been checking one possibility and quickly killed the power, praying FORMAT hadn't reached the section of the disk I was interested in. I was relieved when Debug said the data was still there. Then I hit the wrong key and saw what looked like the first file on my freshly formatted disk.

My reaction? Utter disbelief. What we need to discover is often effectively blocked by what we know already. FORMAT meant FORMAT, a deadly, permanent, total loss of stored information. Format itself said so: ALL DATA WILL BE LOST! Or at least some versions said that.

What to do? Format the disk again, and let it run to the end, I decided. I *wanted* that data to disappear the way it was supposed to,—the way the rules said it should. When it wouldn't, I decided I must have a bad copy of Debug. Then I thought I must have a defective Format, so I got out the DOS diskette. Finally I decided the computer must be malfunctioning. I spent the rest of that day tearing apart my machine, reassembling it, reloading my backups, formatting, debugging, exhausting all the plausible explanations until the implausible was the only one left: FORMAT on a hard disk does *not* erase data.

It was more or less simple to write something that copied the portion of the disk Format does clobber, the FATs and root Directory, so they could be replaced when needed. After the Mace Utilities became well-known, a number of people quickly produced a similar feature. It was to take me another year to figure out how to recover from a Format without a copy of the FAT or root directory, but once that initial discovery was made, the rest was just a matter of piecing together the puzzle.

After the disbelief came the deep satisfaction that every compulsive know-it-all longs for but few ever achieve: to know something exclusively first. Afterwards would come the depression when no one believed me. There was also some anger when I recollected the several times since installing my hard disk when I destroyed—I thought—weeks of work by not paying close attention to which drive I was on when I typed FORMAT. Why hadn't anyone told me? Why hadn't IBM or Microsoft provided the means for backing out of this situation? Certainly somewhere, *someone* knew what I knew, if only the programmer who had written the FORMAT utility. Was this his or her idea of a practical joke?

It turned out later that a number of people knew this already, that a hard disk Format was "logical" rather than "physical". The thing was, none of them saw particular value or significance in this fact. Computer professionals—people who make their living programming computers for others to use—are steeped in the mainframe tradition, where "computer operators" make regular backups and do other dirty odd jobs, such as format disks. Programmers' couldn't understand why anyone would *need* to recover from a FORMAT.

Of course, I was looking at the problem as an outsider, a computer user, a point of view I still cherish. I had stumbled backwards across a poorly marked border, where the new world of desktop computers, as most of us know it, extends away from the traditional land of mainframes, minis, and the cultivated data-processing elite who maintain them. We are to them as Americans to the English, —in the words of Oscar Wilde, "Two peoples separated by a common language."

I was to discover over the next several years, the extent to which the desktop computing world was influenced by those who longed for their mainframe roots, and how that influence threatens at times to prevail. But that's another story.

This book is about the other discoveries, the ones that followed my stumbling upon the truth about DOS Format. In the two years it took to convince other people I wasn't nuts, I spent my time tracking down other possibilities for recovering presumably lost files. In some cases I was treading ground already broken by Peter Norton, but there were things he had overlooked, some of them crucial.

The tide of belief shifted suddenly, unexpectedly in my favor in March 1986, when columnist John Dvorak screwed up a file one day. Out of curiosity, he picked a copy of Mace off a mountain of other packages sent in blind hope—software he would never find time to look at—and said, "This looks interesting." Because he said so in print, people began to believe.

The last two years have seen something akin to learning surgery under battlefield conditions—telepathic surgery, in many cases, as the nature of the damage and reconstruction took place long distance over the phone. A good measure of what is contained in these pages was learned while applying the basic discoveries of the quiet years to the real disasters of the last two. I owe a great deal to those of you who endured the learning along with the recovery, and to those of you I learned from but was unable to help.

What This Book Is About

Everything I have learned in the last five years about recovering lost or damaged data is recorded here. While any programmer who reads it would learn enough to write his or her own software, that's not my purpose. I want the common IBM compatible user to know when and how to use existing commercial software to recover.

This is a reference book. While you could, and should, read the early sections for the general knowledge they impart, that isn't strictly necessary. The heart of the book is the recovery section and the index at the back. You can look up any error message or key word alphabetically in the index and find everything you need to know to carry out complete recovery in one place in the recovery section.

This book isn't meant to replace the manuals that come with the software I talk about. They are likely to contain more timely information, about what key to press, for example, in this version of Mace Utilities or Norton Utilities to UnDelete a file. But the basic concerns remain the same, and there's rarely enough guidance in the user manuals for you to understand the how, the why, and, most importantly, why not, of recovering lost or damaged data. A lot can go wrong on the road to recovery. My purpose is to steer you around the obstacles and down the path to success.

I not only talk about my own software, I talk about Peter Norton's, Central Point Software's, and others. While I'm not impartial, I'm not as biased as you might think. No one software package is *ideal*, mine included. Where someone else's does the job, I say so. In fact all three companies regularly refer customers to one another when they believe they can't help but the other can, with the worst cases usually coming to me personally.

My purpose here, though, is to tell you how to use the software you already own to do the job. In many cases that means DOS. In some instances that means a product published by me, because it is the only alternative I know of as I write. I don't offer my instruction for Norton and PC Tools as an alternative to their manuals, but as additional guidance around the many inevitable pitfalls.

One of the earliest owners of Mace began by first asking, skeptically, "If you really can recover from an accidental FORMAT, how come Peter Norton didn't think of it?"

It suggests the level of reverence people held and still hold for Peter. Bear in mind, until Mace Utilities, data recovery on PCs meant Peter Norton's Unerase. Beyond that, if you didn't have a good backup you were stuck.

The answer to the customer's question was, and is "I don't know. Perhaps he never had to. I did."

Much of what I myself thought impossible in the past now has a solution. Just last week, in conversation with Barry Simon, a most-super-user and writer about PCs, I suddenly realized it was possible to fix cross-linked files, a problem that has bugged me and others for years. It simply took time for all the pieces to come together and for the right person to ask the right question at the right time. That's what discovery is, long slow hard and often painful struggle towards sudden effortless leaps.

Data recovery is, after all, a specialty. Not my chosen profession. Still, I've got a lot of practice in the past few years Theory follows experience and not the other way around. This is a compendium of my experience.

How This Book Is Organized

First, there is advice on staying out of trouble—always the wisest strategy. Next comes an explanation of hard and floppy disks, how they work and fail.

Then comes a section on DOS, the DOS commands used to prepare a disk, and an explanation of the errors they can produce. This will give you some valuable insight into the way things work and don't work, and point you toward recovery from various DOS mistakes and errors.

Finally, there is the Recovery section. This details alphabetically by problem everything you need in the way of software, knowledge, and procedures to recover from every conceivable disk disaster short of outright physical destruction of the disk.

Last is a comprehensive index, elaborately cross-referenced by key word. You should be able to find your way directly from there to any recovery topic.

Chapter 1
Basics

Staying Out of Trouble

There are only two types of computer user; those who have lost valuable data and those who are about to.

I'll keep the sermon short: She who doesn't backup her data is lost. He too. Nothing, other than backup copies, can forestall the day when weeks, months, or years of valuable work vanishes forever. It can be as stunning as learning your house just burned down with all your possessions. I'm not exaggerating. Just because it's compact and invisible doesn't lessen the value of the work stored on your computer. Careers have been ended, companies crippled, millions of dollars lost due to the failure to adequately safeguard information with backup copies. Think about what it would take to do the work all over again from scratch?

Below, I tell you what it'll take to ensure that fateful day never comes. Only you can decide what degree of risk is most comfortable for you.

Tape Backup

This is still the most common, effective, and reliable way to preserve data. If you are serious about preventing data loss, you'll keep five tapes, one for each day of the week, and rotate them for a daily backup. Likewise you'll have a tape for each month and each year. This assures you'll never lose more than a day's work under normal circumstances. In extreme cases, you can bring everything back to the last known good week or month. If you do serious work on your computer, I guarantee one day you'll long for a tape archive.

If you run a Local Area Network, tape backup is essential. I use a Maynard Maynstream. It's fast, reliable, supports our StarLAN network, and has very good software. That's the key, the software. A lot of good tape equipment comes with deplorable software. Make sure whatever you get comes with a 30-day money-back guarantee, and don't be afraid to take it back if you can't get it to work right. Don't be cowed by a salesman who makes you feel dumb; tape backup software should be easy to use and bulletproof. If you can't make it work consistently on your equipment, it is useless or even *dangerous*! Try something else.

Many tape drives come with resident software that'll perform unattended backups at a specific time every day. If your machine is on all the time, this may be appropriate for you, but someone will still have to ensure the tape is changed and verify daily that all is working properly.

Bernoulli Cartridges

We also use a 20 + 20 Bernoulli box and the DOS XCOPY command for backup storage. The Bernoulli provides storage on convenient removable cartridges and performance close to that of a hard disk. While we've never had a problem with our backups, Bernoulli cartridges do wear out when used as a hard disk substitute for everyday work. I don't recommend them for that. As a backup or archival medium, however, they have the advantage of looking to the user like any other drive. Because you understand what they are doing, you are less intimidated. Trust leads to frequent use. The best equipment in the world is worthless if you're shy of it.

Floppy Backup

This is a tough one. Normally I would say go with the company with the longer track record; experience being everything in the software world. But the truth is, you can't tell. The people who originate a product rarely survive its success. (Norton and I are exceptions.) They quit, sell out, or are shoved out by partners and investors, and they take their wisdom with them. The product remains, embodying the ideas of successive generations of hired programmers, but there are often unresolved gaps in performance because no one is ever around long enough to see the whole picture in light of past experience.

I have never had a floppy backup program that didn't fail me. I have friends who swear by DOS, Fastback, CoreFast, and half a dozen others of less repute. That doesn't mean they will or won't work for you. You're going to have to experiment.

All the "fast" backup programs use DMA transfer to work their magic. DMA means direct memory access, and refers to chips inside the computer that can send data to and from memory without using the central processor. This means the program can be sending data to the diskette in A: while it talks to you about getting B: ready. The machine is literally doing two things at once, and because data is always on the move, the backup process streams along. The bad news here is that some machines have faulty DMA chips. You must run a test program to determine if your machine will support fast backups. There are other subtle drive and memory problems you may not be aware of during everyday use that will render fast backup programs useless, and you'll never know until the day you need to restore.

What to do? COPY or XCOPY your valuable data to floppies or some other drive first, then backup and restore a few times. Try putting a pinhole through one of the backup copies and see what happens to the restore operation. I'm serious! If one disk goes bad and the restore operation grinds to a halt on that disk, you're stuck. One of the most crushing feelings in computing is the discovery that your backup is no good.

If you can't get a program to work, call the publisher or your dealer for support. If they can't resolve the problem, return it and ask for a competing product or your money back. There is not a reputable dealer or publisher who won't refund your purchase if he can't make the software run as advertised on your machine to your satisfaction.

UPS—Uninterruptable Power Supply

This is a battery in a box, and they've gotten slim, attractive, and less expensive recently—under $500 for one that supports an AT class machine. Don't be confused by power filters and line conditioners, which often look like a UPS in ads, only cheaper. Power filters and line conditioners serve to smooth out turbulent power coming from your wall socket; they do not replace it when it dries up.

If you suffer frequent power outages, a UPS is a must. It will keep your computer humming for 10 minutes to an hour after the power goes out. When selecting the time duration of a UPS, what you have to decide is whether you just need time to gracefully exit your application and shut the machine down yourself, or if it's important to go on computing as long as possible.

The difference is price, and the governing factor is the amp/hour rating of the UPS and how much equipment you want to plug in, as well as how many boards you have installed inside your computer. Explain to your dealer what you have and ask how long each UPS model will run that equipment. If he can't answer, find another dealer, call the manufacturer, or check your computer magazines for a product comparison.

Once you get a UPS, let it charge up for a day, then test it. And remember, it may take a day for the UPS to recover from a single use. Check the recovery times in the manual or with the manufacturer.

UPS Software

This is an interesting category of software. It includes Bookmark, Deja View and POP included in Mace Utilities 5.0 Gold.

These programs periodically take a snapshot of everything in your computer's memory—the part that vanishes when the power goes out. They can then restore memory to the same state it was in at that moment. The presumption is you were doing something and had not recently saved the work to disk. You recover by asking the software to put everything back in memory, placing the machine in the same state it was in when the last snapshot was taken.

If you can afford a real UPS, buy it. These programs don't deal with changes to the disk and don't guarantee perfect recovery the way an orderly shutdown would.

Again, test them under field conditions. Work your way into the middle of something you're prepared to lose, reach down and pull the plug out of the wall. Restoring should give you full and normal use of the machine. If not, don't rely on this software in the future.

Surge Protectors

If you can see the line that runs from the pole to your house and electrical storms are known to happen overhead, you're a candidate for surge protection. These devices are designed to stop a lightning bolt, or some dramatic electrical event in your municipal power supply, from entering your computer and quite literally frying its brains. Instead, you want the "event" to fry the relatively inexpensive surge protector.

All surge protectors are not created equal, either in price or performance. They range in price from $5 to over $150 and there is not always a direct connection between price and performance. The major computer magazines regularly run comparative tests of surge protectors; follow their conclusions.

Power Line Filters

Similar to surge protectors, but generally more expensive, these devices smooth out peaks and valleys in the voltage delivered at the wall socket. Even in an ordinary home or office, the operation of major appliances can dramatically affect the power supplied to your computer. This can lead to seemingly random failures, glitches, and gremlins. If the lights flicker, you may have "dirty" power. A line filter will steady up the juice. Some even contain batteries to "pick up" voltages during sags and brown-outs, but they won't run the computer during a total failure or extended brown-out. Only a real UPS will do that.

Viruses, Vaccines, and Flu shots

A computer virus or flu is not a natural disease. It is the product of a sick mind, a malignant piece of computer code attached to an otherwise harmless program. When you run an infected application the viral code takes control and searches the disk for new files to attach itself to. The system files, IBMBIO.COM, IBMDOS.COM, and COMMAND.COM are favorite targets. Periodically, the viral code takes control and destroys information on your disk—sometimes a little bit at a time, sometimes all at once.

Naturally, a whole industry has sprung up to service people who dread computer flu. Vaccine programs exist that will help detect and defend against many forms of virus, some costing several hundred dollars. There is a public-domain program, Flu-shot, that is excellent and free, though a ten dollar donation to the authors is requested. Mace Vaccine is included in Mace Utilities and available separate for $20. Both programs are listed in the back of the book, and both have benefits that justify them even if you don't copy or download software—these being the only routes of infection.

Most vaccines and flu shots are designed to warn you when unusual attempts are made to access vital disk areas and system files, not just by a computer flu or virus, but by any application that has no business modifying these vital areas of your disk. You can also raise the protection level to prevent any unauthorized access outside of DOS. This will stop any of the current viruses and flus before they stop you.

Understand that the people who make these things are clever and we haven't seen their worst. We're clever too, and will keep improving the vaccine. We can only hope they'll tire of this malicious nonsense before we do.

It has been brutally noted that computer viruses are to software piracy what AIDS is to free sex—a convincing argument against. The best way to avoid giving your computer a virus is to avoid copying software. Use only freshly unpackaged originals to install. If you are given software, or download it, consider it suspect and be certain to run your protection software in its highest protection mode before running the new application for the first time.

For every person whose data succumbs to computer flu, a thousand others will be stricken by more or less ordinary applications gone haywire due to conflicts with other hardware or software. Flu-shot and Mace Vaccine will halt these honest but lethal attempts on your data too. That is reason enough to have them installed on your machine.

If you do believe you're the victim of some villainous program, I'd like to know about it. A free copy of Mace Vaccine goes to anyone who uncovers a new strain of computer flu or virus.

Mace, Norton, PC-Tools

All three packages contain programs that make automatic backups of critical areas of the hard disk. When installed they can make recovery from accidentally deleted files, FORMAT, or other disasters relatively simple, automatic, and perfect or near perfect. They'll help you recover after the fact too, and unless you have rigorous backup habits it's really foolish not to have one of them installed.

Hard Disks

It is a classic "black box": You put data in, you get data out, a light blinks. It can cost anywhere from several hundreds to several thousands of dollars. What it looks like inside, how it works, and why it fails remain a mystery guarded by the dire warning: "Warranty void if seal is broken."

As with so many other aspects of a microcomputer, the "licensed" software and the microchips themselves, miniscule, glued enigmatically inside the black caterpillar packaging, hard disks seem to defy ownership, right down to the queer #8 Torx machine screws used to assemble them. While for the most part no one set out intentionally to mystify how it all works, the effect is the same and there is a great deal of resistance to de-mystification. It is worth a lot of money to understand how computers and disks work, and few people who are in a position to know get paid for explaining.

While it's not easy to make a hard disk, it's not hard to understand how they work—and fail. It's all based on magnetism. Inside the box a motor spins a stack of flat metal disks mounted on an axle at 3600 revolutions per minute. The disks are coated with an oxide similar to what you see on magnetic tape used in stereos and video recorders. Also inside the box are electromagnets, one for each disk surface. Arranged like fingers at the end of a mechanical hand, these can be swung between the spinning platters to record and read information.

That's the easy part, motors, platters, and magnets. Simple? It has to be. We mean to cram an incredible amount of information into that very small space, and do it quickly and reliably, over and over, often round the clock for years. This demand is what requires clever engineering.

If you've ever seen the old Mr. Wizard trick of sprinkling iron filings on a sheet of paper, then bringing a magnet up underneath, you'll appreciate one of the fundamental properties (and problems) associated with hard disk design. Lines of magnetic force don't form straight and parallel lines. They tend to spread out. Only very near the pole of the magnet are they more or less dense and parallel. So it is when designing a hard disk the engineers try to get the recording heads as close as possible to the surface they want to record on. In fact, inside most hard disks the heads "fly" half the thickness of a human hair off the recording surface. And they *are* flying. At 3600 rpm, the disk passing under the head generates quite a wind, 80 miles an hour at the outermost edge—a hurricane. The recording head is not simply holding position in one place; it is constantly being flicked back and forth from the outer edge inwards towards the hub and back, seeking, reading, and writing one of the hundreds of concentric circles where data is stored. So within the hurricane the flying head creates its own additional turbulence as it flutters, sometimes over a hundred times a second, in search of data.

We're not talking about a Boeing 747 here; this is an object the thickness of a playing card weighing a fraction of an ounce. Two of them have to fit in every gap between the stacked platters. Of course, the tighter the stack the more platters (and data) you can get inside the box. The lighter the heads the easier it is to flick them from track to track, making the disk access data faster. The smaller the recording head the finer the magnetic field, so you can get the concentric circles closer together and more data per platter. It follows, of course, that the smaller, thinner, and lighter you make the recording head and the finger on which it's mounted, the more fragile and flimsy it becomes, making it prone to twist, vibrate, and flutter in that turbulent hurricane wind, and less able to hold position exactly half a hair above the disk. Too far away and the tiny magnetic field will not record. Too close and . . . well, they're not called *hard* disks for nothing.

It doesn't take much imagination to visualize what is popularly and accurately termed a "head crash." The recording head, which is really a tiny electromagnet "printed" in the end of a flat finger of composite material, such as carbon fiber, plows into the oxide coating at 80 miles per hour, or bangs off a harder "plated media" surface. Where it leaves a furrow in the oxide, recorded information is scraped away, perhaps completely. The experience doesn't improve the recording head either. The amazing thing is that it happens and things continue to work normally. A little lubricant applied over the oxide helps on most disks.

Head impact is also lessened by the fact that the wind inside the box tends to blow away from the surface of the disk. Because the head relies on this updraft to stay out of danger, the greatest risk of a head crash comes when power is applied and the disk is starting up, or slowing down when the power is turned off, and the protective updraft suddenly weakens and dies. Of course, this is precisely when you are pushing yourself away, or tucking your legs in at the start of the day, jiggling and banging the desk. To counter this many manufacturers automatically retract and lock the heads to a safe area when the power cuts off and don't unlock them until the disk comes up to speed. You can achieve something like the same protection by going easy on the furniture and running a head parking program before shutdown. Park programs typically move the heads to a track near the inner hub where data is never stored.

When the platters finally stop spinning, the heads on many hard disks come naturally to rest against the surface of the platter. They're designed that way. Of course, slamming the machine around while the power is off is likely to set up a tap dance between the heads and the platters, and is not recommended. But there is nothing particularly dangerous about the heads touching the inert disk.

One thing I've neglected to mention thus far is heat. The motor that drives the platters, the motor that flicks the heads, the chips attached to the drive, not to mention the chips that make up your computer itself and the boards added in, all generate heat. As with most things, the parts inside the drive expand as heat is added. A drive that begins at 55 degrees in the morning can be operating at well above 100 degrees by late afternoon. This thermal cycling is compounded by placing the computer where air can't circulate, or people failing to replace the metal plates that block the rear slots in the computer case when cards are removed. As a result, the platters can grow quite warm. The heat expansion of platters and positioning mechanisms is subtle. Remember we are not talking about large-scale events but distances measured in fractions of a hair. Engineering the control and flow of heat inside a hard disk is a major task. A poor job resulted in extraordinary failure rates for the CMI disk IBM shipped with its first 6 MHz ATs. Excess heat, or excess thermal cycling from very hot to very cold and back, can lead to failure. If your computer is located where temperatures vary more than 25 degrees in a day, you might consider leaving it on all the time.

Finally, there's the matter of clean air. That's why the whole thing's assembled and sealed in an ultraclean environment and the main reason you shouldn't open it up. A speck of dust inside a hard disk is equivalent to a barrel falling off a truck on a rush hour freeway. The only thing in doubt is the extent of the havoc it will create.

I should point out before someone irately corrects me that hard disks are also sealed for safety and liability reasons. The platters and fingers supporting the heads are brittle and can shatter. You wouldn't want to stand over an open hard disk while it was running without exercising some caution. Not that you couldn't get away with just pulling the cover off right inside your PC, but one day you'd pay for your boldness.

Problems

Hard disks usually fail in one of four major ways:

1. Often the main motor bearings begin to chirp, then scream, then freeze up; the disk does not even spin when power is applied. Backup your data before the chirp reaches a scream, because you're going to lose the disk and everything on it.

2. Another common form of death is head failure. When it happens, it's not subtle. You'll get **Abort Retry** messages from DOS, possibly even an invalid drive specification warning. When you run diagnostic software like Mace Diagnose or HTEST, all the errors will show up on the same head, while everything else tests fine. The read/write head may be damaged from a head crash or grit inside the drive, or it may have broken off altogether. You can recover some data but the bigger the file the more likely recovery is to be fragmentary.

3. A third common mode of failure is creeping paralysis. **Abort Retry** errors become more and more frequent. Low-level formatting will make the problem go away, but only temporarily. Running a program like Mace Remedy will lock out the bad sectors and keep DOS from using the faulty areas. The key here is stability. If you get some bad sectors and Remedy locks them out and no more appear, this is normal. If the errors never stop, the drive is failing and you should prepare to buy a new one. Meanwhile, backup your valuable data regularly.

4. The last major failure is electronic. A chip on the logic board attached to your drive is going bad. This is the one drive hardware failure that any amateur who isn't a klutz can hope to cure. Usually it results in Sector or Address not found messages from DOS. I describe later in the Recovery section when and how to go about replacing this board.

Hard Disk Controllers

Much of what you probably ascribe to the hard disk in the way of powers and problems is really dependent on the controller board through which it

lllBradyLine

Insights into tomorrow's technology from the authors and editors of Brady Books.

You rely on Brady's bestselling computer books for up-to-date information about high technology. Now turn to BradyLine for the details behind the titles.

Find out what new trends in technology spark Brady's authors and editors. Read about what they're working on, and predicting, for the future. Get to know the authors through interviews and profiles, and get to know each other through your questions and comments.

BradyLine keeps you ahead of the trends with the stories behind the latest computer developments. Informative previews of forthcoming books and excerpts from new titles keep you apprised of what's going on in the fields that interest you most.

- Peter Norton on operating systems
- Jim Seymour on business productivity
- Jerry Daniels, Mary Jane Mara, Robert Eckhardt, and Cynthia Harriman on Macintosh development, productivity, and connectivity

Get the Spark. Get BradyLine.

Published quarterly, beginning with the Summer 1988 issue. Free exclusively to our customers. Just fill out and mail this card to begin your subscription.

Name _____

Address _____

City _____ State _____ Zip _____

Name of Book Purchased _____

Date of Purchase _____

Where was this book purchased?   *(circle one)*

     Retail Store   Computer Store   Mail Order

F R E E

Mail this card for your free subscription to BradyLine

Brady Books
One Gulf+Western Plaza
New York, NY 10023

receives data from DOS. The hard disk itself is just a recording device. It has connectors on the back that conform to an industry standard. Until recently this was the ST (for Shugart Technologies) 412 or 506 standard. Among other things, this standard describes which electronic signal appears where on the connector, what it does, and how much data the drive can send or receive at a maximum in a given length of time. What the disk actually receives, how fast, and where it will be placed is determined by DOS and the controller board.

The hard disk controller handles the task of formatting the disk for later use, encoding the data it receives from DOS, instructing the hard disk where to place the read/write heads, writing or reading the data, verifying it, correcting any errors, and reporting back to DOS with the data and status concerning success or failure. While relations between DOS and ST 412 or 506 drives are fixed standards, what happens in between is up to each controller manufacturer, and so is the recording scheme. Consequently, controller cards from different manufacturers should not be considered interchangeable. In practice many are, but that isn't to be relied on unless you've tested and determined for yourself it works.

Many, but not all, hard disk controllers replace the disk BIOS that comes with your machine. They do this electronically, by changing an address where DOS looks for the program code it uses to transact business through the controller with the disk. I mention this because it is a major pitfall to adding third-party controllers to existing computers. When you add a controller you unwittingly alter a major component of the way your machine works, the Basic Input Output System code. The BIOS does clever things, and writing a compatible one is tricky business. In short, you may introduce not just a new controller, but new bugs into your computer that will one day cause strange behavior.

A classic case was the recent discovery that PC DOS 3.3 didn't work on some compatibles. People suddenly began to see **General Failure** messages from their hard disks. It turned out that IBM had implemented a speedup feature in DOS that used multisector reads. The IBM BIOS has always supported this feature, though it had never before been used. Some compatibles and controller boards had the code, but it was buggy. Because it had never been used, no one realized the error was there until they converted to PC-DOS 3.3. Thanks to a good friend, Dave Hoagland, the problem was identified, isolated, and a fix made available. But this is the elusive sort of BIOS related problem that can drive unsophisticated users nuts.

Many weren't even aware that they had a third-party controller in their otherwise "true blue" computer.

There are all sorts of variations between controller manufacturers. Some controllers require you to move little plastic blocks, called Berg jumpers, from one set of pins to another to tell it what size or model drive is attached. Some controllers are "auto-config" and take the information supplied by a low-level formatter and write it to the beginning of the disk as part of the format information. (Some cards have a special, built-in formatter you run through DOS Debug.) Some let you split one physical drive to look like two drives. Some are three to six times more efficient than others at moving data to and from the disk.

All controllers ultimately wear out, and when they do you need to determine whether it is the controller or the hard disk that failed. The standard procedure is to try a known, good, identical controller in its place. Roughly a third of all disk failures I hear about are actually *controller failures*. Good controllers are $100–$150 new. Good hard disks are two to three times that price. And there's also the cost of your lost data. Read the recovery section, but always, before you give up or begin to do something dramatic to your hard disk, make sure the controller is good.

ESDI, SCSI, and RLL

Enhanced Small Device Interface, ESDI for short, is a recent alternative to the old ST 506 standard. There are three things you need to know. IBM, Compaq, and other major manufacturers use it in their new, high-priced, large-capacity machines. It moves data more efficiently from computer to disk and back, chiefly because of modern design and the fact that what used to be up to the controller card is now built-in to the hard disk itself. Which means, finally, you can't plug just any old hard disk into an ESDI controller. Third-party ESDI controller cards and hard disks are available and you can install them in most compatibles in place of the existing disk and controller combination. Not all current low-level test software works with all ESDI controlled drives. Check with the publisher before you try it. Programs such as Mace, Norton, and PC-Tools, however, work just fine.

SCSI, pronounced "scuzzy," is shorthand for Small Computer Standard Interface. It is another "standard" for attaching all sorts of devices, of which hard disks are just one category, to your computer. Again, third-party SCSI controller cards and hard disks are available and you can install them in most compatibles in place of the existing disk and controller combination. Not all current low-level test software works with all SCSI controlled drives. Check with the publisher before you try it. Again, programs such as Mace, Norton, and PC-Tools work fine.

ESDI and SCSI, like the other standards I've mentioned, simply define the electronic signals that appear on a physical connector and the maximum volume of information you can expect to transfer in a given time. What the interface is used for—more important, what information and what form it takes as it passes through the standard interface—is up to each manufacturer. ESDI and SCSI can even talk to each other, when some clever engineers work up a circuit to translate.

RLL, short for Run Length Limited encoding, describes the actual pattern of information recorded on the disk. It has nothing to do with ESDI or SCSI except that some ESDI and SCSI controllers use RLL encoding, while some use the older MFM form of encoding.

A disk controller doesn't really sense whether an area of the disk is magnetized as a north or south pole; detection is too uncertain. Instead it detects the transition from one polarity to the other. Even that is no easy task at the scale and speeds at which the disk operates so data are encoded. RLL and MFM refer to the encoding scheme. Each scheme dictates that the changes in polarity can only take place at certain times and in certain specified patterns for the controller to interpret them as data. What the code scheme seeks to do is eliminate patterns where there are too many transitions from north to south and back in a given time. No mystery here: it's easier on quick examination to tell the difference between 100100 and 100001 than it is between 101010 and 101101. Data encoding takes advantage of that recognition factor.

RLL, pioneered by IBM over a decade ago, uses a longer code, but one that is more easily detected than the older MFM scheme. Consequently data can be packed more densely on the disk and still be accurately read. Fifty percent more data is common to the most popular RLL scheme, known as 2,7 RLL. Hence the "27" on many hard disk controller part numbers. There is also a 3,11 RLL scheme, called ERLL, that doubles disk capacity.

So, why not put RLL or ERLL controllers in all our machines and double disk capacity? Because most older hard disks just won't reliably handle the higher data density and increased transfer rate. I said *reliably*. You may get it to work, but not all the time. The failure rate at six months for the first generation of RLL controllers and disks was somewhere between 25 and 50 percent. Great for practicing your data recovery skills.

Can it work? Absolutely! The Plus Development HardCard is one of the most reliable devices on the market and it is an RLL drive. It was also designed as a unit, controller and drive tuned to work together. Priam has been shipping extremely reliable RLL drive and controller combinations for some time. And the OMTI RLL controllers (same chips as the Plus HardCard) work superbly with drives that are manufactured to support RLL. OMTI and other RLL controllers may work with other non-RLL certified drives too, but that is something you have to prove to yourself by running the risk. It is generally sound policy to buy RLL controller and drive combinations from a single manufacturer. Next best is to consult the drive manufacturer about which RLL controllers work best with their drives—drive manufacturers tend to be conservative, and so should you.

As I mentioned above, many RLL controllers are what is termed auto-config. They record the number of heads, tracks, and other data about the physical characteristics of the drive *on* the drive itself, as part of the format information on track 0 during preparation with the low-level formatter. How they do this is different for each manufacturer, consequently it is not a good idea to run hard disk diagnostic utilities against track 0 when using these controllers. The software may louse up the configuration data and your controller will no longer recognize your drive. Recovery from this disaster is covered later in the book. In the meantime, how do you know what kind of controller you have? If you don't have the controller literature you don't know. You could call the manufacturer, or you could exercise restraint playing around with disk diagnostic software, or both.

Low-Level Format

Before a hard disk leaves the factory it is completely erased. Not only does it not contain any data, it doesn't even contain enough information to begin storing data. That's because the disk manufacturer has no way of knowing what hard disk controller will be attached to the drive. While the connector that attaches the drive to the controller board is standard, the way controllers encode data onto the drive isn't. So, life as a storage device begins for each hard disk with a disk controller level format.

Most of you never see this step. Your dealer or hard disk vendor took care of it. You should however understand the process, as it affects performance and has implications for failure and recovery.

Low-level format is accomplished with the manufacturer's disk diagnostics, or a program built into the disk controller and accessed through DOS DEBUG, or third-party software such as HFORMAT, SPEEDSTOR, and others listed in the back of the book. In order to make use of the disk, the format program instructs the controller to format the disk one surface at a time, dividing up each side of each platter into concentric rings, known as tracks, and breaking up each ring into manageable chunks, called sectors, separated by very small gaps.

A sector begins with a unique pattern that helps the disk controller divine that this is the start of something. Then comes some housekeeping information, which includes the address number of the head, track, and sector, then a block of dummy information, followed by a number known as a checksum, which is computed from the contents of the data. After a gap, in which nothing is recorded, the next sector begins. It is this format information that takes up the difference between the *capacity* and the *formatted capacity* you see in some advertisements.

Most hard disks are formatted with 17 sectors per track and each sector contains 512 bytes of information. But these numbers aren't written in stone, or DOS. The new IBM PS/2 series computers support larger sector sizes and RLL controllers commonly format as many as 37 sectors per track—all in anticipation of very large capacity drives. Programs that allow you to break the 32 megabyte barrier, such as VFeature and Speedstor, may appear to fiddle with sector size when you configure them, but they don't change the disk. Sector size is still 512. They simply lie to DOS.

Besides laying down format information, a controller level format does two other things of note. First, it sets the interleave, which I'll explain shortly. Second, at controller level format time every sector on the disk is tested for the ability to faithfully and reliably record and hold data. Sectors that return errors can be locked out by the controller. This insures that DOS, or any other operating system, can't store data in that sector, no matter how hard it tries.

Related to certification is the *manufacturer's bad-track table*. This is a sticker attached to the outside of the drive that lists the spots on the disk the manufacturer determined to be defective. Virtually all disks have some defects. A list is compiled during testing at the factory and it is much more accurate than anything you or your dealer can determine by running third-party software.

Low-level format programs such as HFORMAT, listed in the back of the book, allow direct entry of the manufacturers bad track information. If this isn't done, you may be able to set up and use the disk, but ultimately those bad spots will surface in the middle of important data. Never take for granted that the bad tracks were entered. Ask your dealer when you pick up the machine, or open the machine and look for that label. If it shows entries, CHKDSK should report some space "unavailable for storage" when DOS is running.

Once all sides of all platters are formatted from the outer rim to the innermost track, and the manufacturer's bad track information entered, this disk is ready, in theory, for DOS FDISK and DOS FORMAT, which I describe next. In reality the wise, conservative thing to do is format the disk many times over the space of several days. Programs like HFORMAT, listed in the back, will do this automatically. Twenty-four hours is a good *minimum* time for low-level formatting. Better to spend the time now looking for bad spots than to have them crop up after data is committed to the disk.

Interleave

This refers to the sequence in which the sectors on a hard disk are organized. The surface of the disk is divided into sectors by a magnetic numbering system. Because the surface of a hard disk moves so rapidly past the drive read/write heads, most computers can't transfer data to and from the disk fast enough to keep up with consecutively numbered sectors (1,2,3 . . .). To allow time for the controller and computer to transfer and process the data being read from the disk, the sectors are usually not numbered sequentially. The sectors are instead *interleaved*, and the sequence of the sectors is called the *interleave factor*. In an AT-class computer, the sectors on the hard disk are often organized with two sectors separating the first and second sectors (1**2**3 . . . an interleave of 1 to 3). For a slower XT-class computer, an interleave of 1 to 6 is common (1*****2*****3 . . .).

When the interleave factor is incorrect, files aren't transferred to and from the hard disk as fast as possible and the overall performance of the computer is slowed. If the interleave is set too fast, the computer won't be able to process the data as rapidly as it appears under the read/write heads and will have to wait for an entire revolution of the hard disk before the data can be read. Conversely, if the interleave factor is too slow, the computer will be ready to read the next sector before it appears and time will be lost waiting for the sector to appear.

Each component can have an effect on the proper interleave factor: some hard disks can read data faster than others, some hard disk controller cards can transfer data faster, and a faster computer can process and transfer data at a faster rate than a slower computer. If you have a "turbo-speed" motherboard or add a turbo board to a computer, you can often use a faster interleave. HOPTIMUM, listed in the back of the book, will determine the correct value and automatically reset the disk for peak performance.

If the interleave is set incorrectly, the disk will work reliably, only slowly. A large number of machines have incorrect interleaves, either because the manufacturer's recommended default is too conservative, or the person who set it up guessed wrong. If you want to test for yourself, I'll send you Marc Kolod's HPERF on a disk for two bucks.

Problems

I want to emphasize that most hard disks have defects. This is normal, though defects should comprise less than 1 percent of available storage. Vendors know this, but also realize that many customers resist buying disks that have defects or *locked-out* areas. So they don't enter manufacturer's bad track information. The customer sees what he wants, a perfect disk. The vendor reasons that if his low-level format program passed the disk, the manufacturer was just being conservative. This is deadly logic, and it will come back to haunt both customer and vendor. Accept that some defects are normal even on a new disk, but insist that all known defects are locked out before using the disk.

Another dangerous practice related to bad spots on the hard disk is endeavoring to "fix" them with software. There are several people making this claim in advertising. Reclaiming bad spots for storage is not impossible. It may even be necessary in the short run, to recover data or to limp along until time or money is available for a replacement. But it is always risky, usually dumb, and ultimately self-defeating. Once a spot is detected as bad, it should be left bad.

FDISK

DOS is shorthand for Disk Operating System. In fact PC- and MS-DOS are only one of many such systems—logical schemes for storing and retrieving data from disks. After a disk has been prepared with a low-level format program to receive data, it is still several steps away from being a DOS disk. It lacks, first off, some indication for the computer of what operating system is on the disk and where.

You are no doubt accustomed to thinking of your PC and PC- or MS-DOS as being inseparable. In fact, the machine will recognize any one of a number of commercial operating systems, including Unix, Venix, Xenix, Pick, Oasys and CP/M-86, not to mention OS/2. All it wants is an entry in what is called the Master Boot Record, indicating where the operating system begins on disk, how much space it occupies, whether it is currently active, and a unique signature character by which it wants to be known. FDISK is the DOS program that fills in this information.

The first thing you should do with FDISK is think before using it. More people, myself included, have lost data from idly poking around with FDISK than from any other disaster, except accidental FORMAT. If your machine is already up and running, delete all copies of FDISK from your hard disk. No one, not even software developers, needs this capability so frequently that he can't hunt up an original DOS diskette and use it from there when necessary. While you're hunting it up, you can think about just what it is you mean to do.

When using FDISK, for the first time or thereafter, always begin with the "View partition information" option. See what's there. This is the one thing FDISK will do for you that is safe: show you the status of the disk.

"No partitions defined," will greet you the first time a disk is initialized or after a disaster. There might be partitions other than DOS on the disk. DOS FDISK won't touch the Master Boot Record (MBR) entries for these other systems, though Marc Kolod's XFDISK will. Some versions of FDISK, however, will let you define a DOS partition that overlaps those other partitions and, eventually, whacks the data stored in them. Do not rely on FDISK to keep you from making this or other disastrous mistakes, rely on your own caution.

"Create DOS partition," is the most commonly used FDISK option. This is the routine that elicits information from you for setting up either a primary DOS area on the disk, or additional secondary partitions.

Primary partitions are the first partition on each physical drive, and may take up all or only part of a physical disk. Secondary partitions allow drives not totally committed to a primary partition to be split into additional partitions, which DOS treats as separate disks and which get their own drive letter.

Regarding the assignment of drive letters, most versions of FDISK (and "AT" SETUP) lie, for the sake of simplicity. Usually FDISK refers to the Primary DOS partition as C: and the next DOS partition as D:. It ain't always so. The rule is: You must have a primary partition on each drive before you can declare a secondary. The first primary DOS partition is C:, no matter which physical drive it is on. If your first disk dies or the Master Boot Record is damaged or erased for some reason, DOS will automatically reassign the second primary partition as C:.

If you have more than one physical drive, the primary DOS partitions on *each* drive are assigned sequentially, C, D, E, etc. When DOS is done lettering the primary partitions on each physical drive, it then goes back and picks up the secondary partitions, starting with the first physical drive. That means, in systems with more than one physical drive installed, C: and D: would, for example, be on separate physical drives, while E: and F: would be the first and second secondary partitions on the same drive as C:, and G: and H: the first and second secondary partitions on the same physical drive as D:.

If you still don't get it, don't worry until recovery day. It all has to do with block device driver installation, which I won't explain. The French filmmaker, Jean Renoir, once said, "There is one thing terrible about human existence, every man has his own good reasons." Enough to say that DOS is more reasonably terrible than any ten men.

With early versions of DOS life was simple: you could only have one DOS partition on a disk and it was limited to 20 megabytes. This was raised to 32 megabytes, then came multiple 32 megabyte partitions, and now up to 24 partitions of up to 512 megabytes, all accomplished with FDISK. As you break the 32 megabyte barrier, however, you may find that some programs no longer work—mostly utility software such as Mace, Norton, and

PC-Tools, or public domain utility software. You'll need to upgrade to the latest editions, or stay under 32 megabytes in partitions where you want to use them.

Once you've decided how to split up the disk, FDISK will endeavor to fill out the MBR, which occupies the outermost top surface of the disk, that is, track 0, head 0. Under DOS 2.x, it takes up one sector, and the DOS partition can start on sector 2. Under DOS 3.x the MBR occupies all of track 0, head 0, and the first DOS partition can (and usually does) start on the next surface, track 0, head 1, sector 1.

The most significant thing to note is that regardless of which DOS version—or which operating system, for that matter—you use, the MBR always comes first. The DOS partition, or partitions, can reside anywhere on the disk, but the MBR must be located on head 0, track 0; there is no alternative position.

It follows that if and when track 0, head 0 becomes unreadable due to corruption, wear, mechanical, or electronic failure, the disk will fail, even if the rest of it is perfectly normal. You will get an "Invalid drive specification" message if you boot from a floppy and try to get onto the disk. DOS FORMAT will fail, low-level format may fail, and so may FDISK.

Most manufacturers recognize the vital importance of track 0, and test and certify it to higher standards than the rest of the disk. DOS FDISK checks to be sure. If it can't read and write to track 0, it won't let you create, or re-create, a DOS partition.

Under DOS major Version 3.x, FDISK goes farther; it writes and reads the areas of the disk where the DOS Boot Record, File Allocation Tables, and Root Directory will go. If they aren't perfect, it won't allow you to create a DOS partition. It even checks the area where the DOS operating system files and COMMAND.COM will be stored—in fact, it gets a little carried away, and tests on out into the data area itself, erasing as it goes. Any errors on this part of the disk will cause FDISK to issue a failure message. Otherwise, it will update the MBR and wait for you to finish before forcing a reboot of the system.

Your machine boots from the partition marked in the MBR as being *active*. Only one partition can be active at a time, and some versions of FDISK don't automatically activate the first DOS partition when you create it. You have to choose the "Change active partition," option and do it yourself, manually. Otherwise, DOS FORMAT fails, cryptically and mysteriously. Always review partition information before exiting FDISK to make sure the first DOS partition shows Status as "A" for active.

The machine only reads the MBR once, when the power is turned on, or the machine is reset, or the Ctrl-Alt-Del keys pressed for a warm boot. Consequently, FDISK forces a reboot after altering the MBR, forcing any changes to take effect.

FDISK Errors

Cannot Read Partition Table

FDISK couldn't read the first sector on head 0, track 0 on the disk where the MBR is located. DOS won't recognize the drive as valid.

Recovery is detailed on page 187.

Cannot Write Partition Table

FDISK couldn't write the first sector on head 0, track 0 on the disk where the MBR is located. DOS won't recognize the drive as valid.

Recovery is detailed on page 187.

Invalid Drive Specification

FDISK couldn't read the first sector on head 0, track 0 on the disk where the MBR is located. DOS won't recognize the drive as valid.

Recovery is detailed on page 187.

No Hard Disk Attached

As far as DOS is concerned, you don't have a hard disk installed in your machine. If you do, it is incorrectly installed or has failed. Normally you would see a 1701 error when you turned the power on, or 17xx, that is, some error number related to hard disks, which is IBM diagnostic category 17.

Recovery is detailed on page 182.

Track 0 Bad—Disk Unusable

FDISK detected an error while reading or writing track 0. It won't use the disk for DOS.

This message has a slightly different nuance for floppies and for DOS FORMAT. Read the section on FORMAT for more facts.

Recovery is detailed on page 187.

Floppy Disks

A floppy disk drive is a cross between a 45-rpm record player and a cassette tape recorder. When you insert a disk and close the drive door, or turn down the latch, a spindle clamps the center hole and begins turning the disk inside its jacket at 300 rpm (360 rpm on 1.2 megabyte and 3½ inch microfloppy diskettes). At the same time, a read/write head similar to that on a cassette recorder is pressed against one or both sides of the disk. The head is a small electromagnet. By turning it on and off the computer magnetizes a thin circular band on the surface of the disk, or senses what was previously written there, first the top surface, then the bottom. Then the heads are moved together to another track and the process repeated.

What you see when you pick up a floppy disk is the package, commonly black (gray or blue for 3½ disks). Beside giving you something to hold on to without touching the disk itself, this jacket holds the disk rigid as it spins and usually contains some form of lining impregnated with cleaning lubricant to keep the surface of the disk free from lint and to insure it rides smoothly under the heads.

The disk itself is visible in the center hole and through the oval cutout on 5¼ disks. On 3½ inch microfloppies the hub is metal, allowing more exact centering and denser recording; the disk is hidden behind a metal or plastic shutter—a weak point of an otherwise superior design. In both cases the "floppy" part is a circular piece of plastic—the "cookie," it's called—coated with an iron compound similar to cassette or video tape and polished smooth. Higher capacity floppies have a different coating that requires more powerful read/write heads, which is one reason you can't use 1.2 megabyte disks in older 360K drives.

The quality of the plastic, the coating, the degree of smoothness to which it is burnished, thickness of the jacket, and quality of the shutter all determine the reliability of the disk and the cost of manufacturing it. In general, cheap disks are inclined to go bad, more expensive disks aren't. The price you pay for economy diskettes often shows up as worn-out heads on the drive itself. Cheap disks, which don't get a final polish, sandpaper the read/write heads to destruction. Most disks fall in the middle in both price and performance. Although manufacturers test each one before packaging, standards vary. The testing machines themselves must be tested with other testing machines in the hands of human beings who often have a bad day. In a thousand, perhaps a handful of defective disks will slip through. Occasionally they will all end up in the box you bought.

Floppy disks are not fragile. Despite the many taboos surrounding the care and handling of floppy disks, the fact remains: they're tough, durable, and reliable. It's difficult to deliberately ruin one, unless you poke or shoot it full of holes, or thumb-tack it to your bulletin board. Running it through the airport baggage check won't erase it—it's not x-rays, but the powerful magnet at the back of the x-ray tube that poses a threat. You're in more danger removing the disks and handing them over the top of the x-ray machine to the operator than leaving them in your bag. The local library is far more lethal, the most common form of book theft protection being a powerful magnet under the checkout counter that sensitizes a magnetic tape strip in the book spine, and wipes out your disks just above. Leaving floppies on top of the t.v. (or your monitor!) is not advised. Don't paper-clip notes to floppies, it crimps the jacket, and you probably got the clip from a cute dispenser that always holds a few handy, sticking up, by means of a magnet! Flexing it or putting a thumbprint on the surface doesn't erase a floppy; it transfers oil and dirt to the read/write heads, which then perform poorly.

In the end, it is *use* more often than abuse that does a floppy in. They do wear out. Also, your drive wears out. Parts need replacing or adjustment. There is diagnostic software available that will tell you if your floppy drive is ailing and needs adjustment. I use Memory Minder from J/M, listed in the back of the book.

One caution about having your floppy drives adjusted: before you do, make certain all your important diskettes are readable on some other machine whose drives aren't being repaired. If the floppy drive you're having repaired has been out of adjustment for some time, all your disks may be a little off. While the poorly-adjusted drive could handle them, a well-adjusted drive might not. It happens too often that someone gets all the drives in the office tuned-up at once and finds afterwards none of them will read the existing data disks. Worse, they can't easily be put back to their old incorrect adjustment.

Most commonly floppy data is lost due to a weary or harassed operator erasing or swapping at the wrong moment, or to ordinary programs driven madcap by some unforeseen combination of keystrokes or resident software.

FORMAT

Floppy Disks

A floppy disk, like a hard disk, arrives with uniformly blank magnetic surfaces. The two-step process of marking out where the data will go, then initializing the DOS areas, is combined for a floppy diskette into one operation.

First the entire diskette is written with format information in a series of concentric, broken circles. Each circle, or track, on each side of the diskette, is recorded as a series of sectors separated by very small gaps. A sector begins with a pattern that helps the disk controller divine that this is the start of something. Then comes some housekeeping information, which includes the address number of the sector, followed by a block of dummy information, and finally a number known as a checksum, which is computed from the contents of the data. After a gap in which nothing is recorded, the next sector begins.

Even after a floppy disk is physically prepared to hold data, the disk isn't ready for use. To make it usable FORMAT must establish a DOS Boot Sector, at least one copy of the File Allocation Table (FAT), and an empty root directory.

The DOS Boot Sector is what the machine uses to bring up the operating system when you turn the power on, or reboot with Ctrl-Alt-Del from a floppy. The machine blindly reads it in and begins executing it as if it were a program. It is, in fact, a small program and contains some important pieces of data specific to DOS and this DOS partition. It records how big the boot sector is, the size and number of FATs, the size of data clusters, how big the root directory is, and what the system files are called. Using this information, the machine reads in the first part of the PC- or MS-DOS operating system, which has the rest of the information and program code necessary to erect a complete DOS structure in memory, load a copy of COMMAND.COM and give you that lovely C> prompt.

Every floppy disk has a DOS Boot Sector, at a minimum for the information about its FATs, root directory, and cluster size. Without a valid DOS Boot Sector on the diskette, the machine won't be able to figure out which of the many possible floppy formats this is.

Right after the DOS Boot Sector comes the first copy of the File Allocation Table. The FAT has one entry for every place on the disk where DOS can store data. When a file is written to diskette, an entry is made in the FAT indicating that area of the diskette is occupied and where the next piece of data will be found, or that this is the end of the file. Thus, files can be (and are) randomly stored wherever space is available—fragmented or if you prefer, segmented.

In a fragmented FAT, one entry points to some distant part of the table, which points to still further distant parts, or perhaps back to some freshly vacated spot near the beginning. While DOS is mentally adept at hopping from one entry to the next while reading a fragmented FAT, your diskette drive is thick-witted. Every hop in the FAT results in a physical hop for the read/write heads on your floppy drive. So, while the segmentation practice maximizes storage efficiency, it can bring data retrieval on a floppy disk to its knees. The cure is to make use of a defragger such as Mace UnFrag, Disk Optimizer, or Vopt and memory caching software such as Mace MCache or others listed in the back of the book.

Each FAT begins with a special entry, the Media Descriptor Byte, that tells DOS, and certain programs like CHKDSK, what sort of diskette this is. The FAT also contains one other special kind of value, which tells DOS not to use a given space because the corresponding area of the disk has a defect of some sort that makes it unreliable for storing data.

While it may have as few as one, and can have many, DOS generally maintains two identical copies of the FAT for each logical drive; in case of physical damage to one copy, it will use the other. But it can't arbitrate between the FATs if they disagree, any more than Solomon could in the Old Testament between the two women who both claimed to be the real mother. In the absence of other information, either could be telling the truth. You, however, may make some more intelligent estimates concerning FATs that disagree and fix such a problem with a disk sector editor.

The Root Directory area always follows the last copy of the FAT. This is the main directory from which all others begin to branch. It is fixed in length and typically holds from 64 to 224 entries, depending on the media type. When it fills up, DOS will report an error and you'll have to delete something to make room. Beyond the Root Directory, data storage extends to the end of the diskette.

DOS FORMAT on a floppy diskette begins by laying down fresh format information and dummy data, then reading it a track at a time. It is looking for sectors that won't accurately retain data or format information. It will mark these locations in the FAT as locked-out; they are unavailable for storage. When it finishes writing and reading, FORMAT writes a new DOS boot sector. It then initializes both FATs by marking their first character with a media descriptor and filling them with zeroes, or locked-out characters where appropriate. Finally, it blanks out the Root Directory area. The diskette is ready for use. Any data that used to be on the disk beyond the Root Directory area is wiped out.

If you specified the /v option on the command line, FORMAT will prompt you to supply a name for the volume, and make a special entry in the root directory. If you specified the /s option on the command line, FORMAT begins by copying the system files from the boot disk. When done formatting, it copies these files to the target disk at the start of the data area. It then creates directory entries for them in the first two slots in the root directory. The system filenames must agree with the names recorded in the DOS Boot Sector, they must be the first two entries in the root, and the data itself must start first on the disk. If any of those conditions aren't met, the disk won't boot. Finally, COMMAND.COM is transferred from the boot disk and you have a bootable system diskette.

If you specified the /b option, the system names are created in the root directory and two dummy files are stored at the beginning of the diskette. These are place-holders. Recall that I said placement was important for the system files. If you record other files onto the diskette and they take up the first part of data storage or the first two slots in the root directory, you can't make that diskette bootable. The /b disk won't boot either, but you can later transfer genuine system files with the SYS command, and the diskette will become bootable because the critical operating system area was reserved at FORMAT time. The only floppy format program that doesn't destroy data is the one that comes with Mace Utilities.

FORMAT

Hard Disks

A hard disk is physically prepared to hold data with a low-level format program, discussed earlier. Afterwards, FDISK is run to establish DOS's rights to all or some of the physical disk, but you're still not ready to begin. To make the DOS partition usable, you must establish a DOS Boot Sector, at least one copy of the File Allocation Table and an empty Root Directory. This is the job of DOS Format.

The DOS Boot Sector is what the Master Boot Record helps point the machine to when you turn the power on or reboot with Ctrl-Alt-Del. The machine blindly reads it in and begins executing it as if it were a program. It is, in fact, a small program and contains some important pieces of data specific to DOS and this DOS partition. It records how big the boot sector is, how many FATs and how big they are, the size of data clusters, how big the root directory is and what the system files are called. Using this information, the machine reads in the first part of the PC- or MS-DOS operating system, which has the rest of the information and program code necessary to erect a complete DOS structure in memory, load a copy of COMMAND.COM and give you that lovely C> prompt.

Each DOS partition, whether Primary or Extended, whether you boot from it or not, has a DOS Boot Sector, at a minimum for the information about its FATs, root directory, and cluster size. Without a valid DOS Boot Sector on the boot drive, usually drive C:, the machine will freeze, or boot into BASIC.

Right after the DOS Boot Sector comes the first copy of the File Allocation Table. The FAT has one entry for every place on the disk where DOS can store data. When a file is written to disk, an entry is made in the FAT indicating that area of the disk is occupied and where the next piece of data will be found, or that this is the end of the file. Thus, files can be (and are) randomly stored wherever space is available—fragmented or if you prefer, segmented.

In a fragmented FAT, one entry points to some distant part of the table. This may point farther on, or perhaps back to some freshly vacated spot near the beginning. While DOS is mentally adept at hopping from one entry to the next while reading a fragmented FAT, your disk is thick-witted. Every hop in the FAT results in a physical hop for the read/write heads on your hard disk. So, while the segmentation practice maximizes storage efficiency, it can bring data retrieval on even the fastest hard disk shaking to its knees. The cure is to make use of a defragger such as Mace UnFrag, Disk Optimizer, or Vopt and memory caching software such as Mace MCache or others listed in the back of the book.

Each FAT begins with a special entry, the Media Descriptor Byte, that tells DOS and certain programs, like CHKDSK, what sort of disk this is. The FAT also contains one other special kind of value, which tells DOS not to use a given space, because the corresponding area of the disk has a defect of some sort that makes it unreliable for storing data.

DOS generally maintains two identical copies of the FAT. In case of physical damage to one copy, it will use the other. But it can't arbitrate between the FATs if they disagree—there are only two, so it is impossible for DOS to say which is correct. You, however, may make some more intelligent estimates concerning FATs that disagree and fix such a problem with a disk sector editor.

After the second copy of the FAT comes the Root Directory area. This is the main directory from which all others begin to branch. It is fixed in length and typically holds a maximum of 512 entries. On larger disks it may hold 1024 entries. When it fills up, DOS will report an error and you'll have to delete something to make room. This normally only affects people who do not know about, or refuse to create subdirectories.

Beyond the Root Directory, data storage extends to the end of the DOS partition. That may mean to the end of the disk or, on a disk with multiple partitions, storage will end on the track number just before the track where next partition's Boot Sector begins.

In most versions, DOS FORMAT begins by *reading* the disk from start to finish. It is looking for sectors marked bad during the low-level format process, or that have gone bad since. It will mark these location in the FAT as locked-out; they are unavailable for storage. When it finishes reading, FORMAT writes a new DOS boot sector. It then initializes both FATs by marking their first character with a media descriptor and filling them with zeroes, or locked-out characters where appropriate. Finally, it blanks out the root directory area. The disk is ready for use. Any data that used to be on the disk beyond the root directory area is still there.

At least three brands of FORMAT that I know of are lethal. They write to the entire surface of the disk, similar to a low-level format. These destructive FORMATs include COMPAQ MS-DOS before 3.21, ATT MS-DOS prior to 3.1 Release 1.01, and Burroughs MS-DOS. They erase the disk.

If you specified the /v option on the command line, FORMAT will prompt you to supply a name for the volume, and make a special entry in the root directory. If you specified the /s option on the command line, FORMAT begins by copying the system files from the boot disk. When done formatting, it copies these files to the target disk at the start of the data area. It then creates directory entries for them in the first two slots in the root directory. The system filenames must agree with the names recorded in the DOS Boot Sector, they must be the first two entries in the root, and the data itself must start first on the disk. If any of those conditions aren't met, the disk won't boot. Finally, COMMAND.COM is transferred from the boot disk, and you have a bootable system disk.

FORMAT Errors

Cannot Format ASSIGNed or SUBSTed Drive

Means what it says. ASSIGN and SUBSTITUTE are tricks, used to make a drive or directory respond to another letter.

Cannot FORMAT a Network Drive

A network drive may or may not be a DOS logical partition. In any case, you can't format them remotely; you are restricted to formatting real local drives.

Disk Unsuitable for System Disk

The area where system files would be stored is marked as defective. The diskette can, however, be used to store data.

Format Failure

Something happened to prevent FORMAT from completing. Usually there will be an accompanying message with more information about the error condition.

Format Not Supported on Drive X:

This usually means you're trying to use DOS FORMAT on a device, such as a Bernoulli Box, which requires its own special format. Typically, such devices also require a "device = *something*" statement in the CONFIG.SYS file before DOS will recognize them and assign a drive letter.

The manufacturer will normally supply a special utility program for formatting his device.

Incorrect DOS Version

The FORMAT version and the version of DOS currently booted don't agree. You may have several copies of FORMAT.COM on your disk, some from earlier versions of DOS. Possibly your PATH command has been altered, and DOS is finding one of these earlier versions.

Look in the directories specified in PATH for copies of FORMAT. Delete the ones whose date-time stamps are the earliest, or copy a new FOR-MAT.COM from the original diskette for the latest version of DOS you own.

Insufficient Memory for System Transfer

You specified the /s option and FORMAT ran out of memory when it tried to load the system files from the boot disk. FORMAT wants to hold both system files and COMMAND.COM in memory.

You probably have resident software that consumes most or all free memory. You can either remove some resident programs and try FORMAT again, or omit the /s option and, when FORMAT completes, use the SYS command to move system files over (remember to copy COMMAND.COM as well, because SYS doesn't.)

Invalid Parameters

You typed something FORMAT doesn't understand, or the parameters you specified on the command line make no sense for the drive designated. For example, you can't format a hard disk as a /8, 320K diskette. You can't format a hard disk with the /b option for later installation of the operating system.

Invalid Drive Specification

The drive specified doesn't exist, has not been initialized, or the MBR has been corrupted.

Invalid Volume ID

This is one of the schemes devised to prevent you from formatting your hard disk accidentally. With some versions of DOS FORMAT, you must supply a valid volume name before it will proceed against a hard disk.

You can determine this by typing VOL at the DOS prompt. If the disk has been corrupted, VOL might return nonsense or even show blanks, which FORMAT refuses to accept. You'll have to FDISK, delete, and re-create the partition.

Non-System Disk, or Disk Error
Replace and Strike Any Key When Ready

You specified the /s option and when FORMAT went looking for the system files on the boot disk, it didn't find them.

You probably removed the system diskette; put it back. You may have to begin formatting from the system diskette.

Parameters Not Compatible

The parameters specified on the command line make no sense for the drive designated. For example, you can't format a hard disk as a /8 320K diskette.

This Partition Is Format-Protected

Zenith includes a DSKSETUP program that allows a hard disk partition to be protected against FORMAT. You'll have to run DSKSETUP again to remove the protection.

Track 0 Bad—Disk Unusable

DOS can't use a disk unless the first track is free of defects. FORMAT detected an error and won't let you use the disk.

Recovery is detailed on page 187.

WARNING, ALL DATA ON NON-REMOVABLE DISK DRIVE X: WILL BE LOST! Proceed with Format (Y/N)?

This only appears when you FORMAT a hard disk that once had data on it. If you press any key other than N, FORMAT will go ahead and re-initialize the disk. See the section on FORMAT for more about what that means.

In many cases, if you kill the power to the machine, or press Ctrl-Alt-Del, no harm at all will be done. If the disk looks good and CHKDSK reports no errors, you probably caught things in the reading stage, and all is well.

Recovery is detailed on page 110.

DOS CHKDSK

This should be the most frequently run program on your machine. Most of you know it as the program that reports free disk and memory space. But its main function is to check the integrity of the file structure, to insure that all the logical references DOS expects when storing and retrieving data are correct.

CHKDSK insures that all directories are readable, and that the nodes . and .. are valid. The . entry, which always appears first in a subdirectory, is an alias for "self," the current directory. .. is an alias for the "parent" directory. If . or .. are damaged or missing, CHKDSK will report errors and may refuse to process any further down that branch of the file structure. In DOS major Version 3.x CHKDSK has the power to repair minor damage to . and .. but most errors require your intervention to correct.

CHKDSK checks each file entry in the directories against the information in the File Allocation Table. It assures that the directory entry points to a valid place in the FAT and that length, as listed in the directory, and disk space, as allocated in the FAT, agree. If they don't, an error is reported. Forbidden are cross-links, that is, double reference in the FAT to the same allocation space on the disk. By definition, each file is an exclusive copy. It occupies its own space on the disk; no matter how redundant the data, it doesn't share information with other files. CHKDSK reports any such occurrence as a cross link. It is powerless, though, to cure cross-links. You must intervene.

Finally, CHKDSK assures that there is a directory reference for every piece of data allocated in the FAT. If not, it reports how many data clusters in how many file chains have been orphaned and asks if you would like them converted to files—that is, directory entries created—or wiped out, to free space.

CHKDSK Confusion

Before continuing, there are two common misperceptions about CHKDSK I'd like to correct:

First, for CHKDSK to do anything other than report, it must be run with the /**F** option (for Fix). If you don't specify /**F**, CHKDSK merely reports what it would do if you specified /**F**.

Second, CHKDSK *.* will report any fragmented files in the current directory, that is, files listed in this directory that have been stored in more than one physical place on the disk. Fragmentation slows disk performance, often dramatically, and should be corrected on a regular basis with a program such as Mace UnFrag or Disk Optimizer. CHKDSK doesn't give you a report of fragmentation for the entire disk, *only* the current directory. While everything else it does is general to the entire file structure, checking for fragmentation (or segmentation, as some call it) is limited to the current directory.

CHKDSK Errors

Allocation Error, Size Adjusted

The size of the file as indicated in the directory disagrees with the amount of space allocated in the File Allocation Table. This is commonly seen in conjunction with cross-linked files. CHKDSK /F will alter the directory size to match the FAT.

Cannot CHDIR to Path—Tree Past This Point Not Processed

A directory is damaged and CHKDSK can't enter that branch of the file structure.

Recovery detailed on page 63.

Cannot CHDIR to Root

CHKDSK couldn't get out of a branch back into the root directory. This may signal a defect in the root directory area on the disk.

Recovery detailed on page 110.

Cannot CHKDSK a Network Drive

CHKDSK won't work against remote drives on a network.

Cannot CHKDSK a SUBSTed or ASSIGNed Drive

CHKDSK won't work on drives created with the DOS substitute or assign features.

CHDIR .. Failed, Trying Alternate Method

After checking the file structure, CHKDSK couldn't get back to the parent directory using .. and will try another route.

Recovery detailed on page 63.

Contains N Noncontiguous Blocks

The current directory contains fragmented files. This condition slows performance, sometimes dramatically, without you knowing it. The cure is to run a defragger, such as Mace UnFrag, Disk Optimizer, or Vopt.

Directory Bad
Convert to File (Y/N)?

DOS doesn't see this as a valid directory entry. CHKDSK /F will convert whatever information is in it to a file, if you say yes, and the message will go away. Say no, and things will be left as they are.

Recovery detailed on page 66.

Disk Error Reading (or Writing) FAT

One of the File Allocation Table sectors is bad. DOS uses the duplicate, if possible.

Recovery detailed on page 110.

. Entry Has Bad Attribute (or Link or Size)

The . ("self") entry is defective. Under DOS major Version 3.x CHKDSK /F will try to fix the problem.

Recovery detailed on page 63.

.. Entry Has Bad Attribute (or Link or Size)

The .. ("parent") entry is defective. Under DOS major Version 3.x CHKDSK /F will try to fix the problem.

Recovery detailed on page 63.

Errors Found, F Parameter Not Specified Corrections Will Not Be Written to Disk

CHKDSK found something wrong, but the /F parameter wasn't used to invoke it. It is merely reporting and won't take any action to alter the disk and correct what it found.

File Allocation Table Bad, Drive X:

Something has damaged the FAT, or the disk wasn't formatted correctly, or isn't a DOS disk.

Recovery detailed on page 110.

File Not Found

The file you specified was not found. Almost always you have misspelled the name, or are in the wrong directory, or on the wrong drive. Sometimes the file may have been renamed or deleted. Or the disk may be freshly formatted or damaged.

Recovery detailed on page 110.

First Cluster Number Is Invalid, Entry Truncated

The file's directory entry contains an invalid pointer to the File Allocation Table. CHKDSK /F will change the length of the file to zero.

Incorrect DOS Version

The version of CHKDSK you are trying to run is different from the version of DOS used to boot the computer. Either you didn't copy new DOS utilities after you SYSed the disk, or you've restored backups with old system utilities. Or perhaps you've changed your PATH command, and it's finding an older copy of CHKDSK.

Insufficient Room in Root Directory
Erase Files in Root and Repeat CHKDSK

You answered "yes" to the "convert to files . . ." message. CHKDSK always recovers files to the root, where there is limited room. The root is now full.

You'll have to copy the .CHK files to some other directory or disk, then delete those in the root and run CHKDSK /F again.

Invalid Cluster, File Truncated

A file's directory entry points to the wrong place in the FAT, or to a corrupted FAT. CHKDSK /F will alter the file's length to zero.

Invalid Current Directory

Something is wrong with the current directory.

Recovery detailed on page 63.

Invalid Drive Specification

The drive specified doesn't exist, at least from DOS's point of view. Either you're mistaken, or the necessary device driver has been removed from CONFIG.SYS, or something has damaged the MBR.

Recovery detailed on page 178.

Invalid Parameters

CHKDSK recognizes /F for *fix*, and /V for *verbose*. Normally, these are declared after any path or filenames. For example CHKDSK *.*/V will print all filenames to the screen (verbosely) as it checks the disk.

X Lost Clusters Found in Y Chains
Convert Lost Chains to Files (Y/N)?

The File Allocation Table indicates something stored on the disk, but no directory entry points to it. CHKDSK /F will give you the option of erasing the FAT and freeing the space, or creating directory entries for the stranded data. Answer **Yes**, and the chains will be converted to files with a .CHK extension in the root directory. Answer **No**, and the disk space will be freed for future storage.

If you didn't specify the /F option, CHKDSK does nothing. You'll get the same message the next time you run it.

Recovery detailed on page 60.

Probable Non-DOS Disk
Continue (Y/N)?

Either the disk wasn't formatted with DOS, or the Media Descriptor recorded on the disk isn't recognized as valid for this version of DOS. Or the Media Descriptor is corrupt.

Recovery detailed on page 103.

Processing Cannot Continue

You need more free memory to run CHKDSK. Remove resident programs and unneeded device drivers.

DELETE and ERASE

DELETE and ERASE are the same thing: they make file entries disappear from your directory, but they don't remove data from the disk.

When you DELete or ERASE a file, DOS replaces the first character of the filename in the directory with a sigma, σ. This tells it the file is deleted but all other directory information remains, most critically, the original length of the file and the File Allocation Table (FAT) entry corresponding to where it was stored physically on the disk.

The FAT is a map of the disk, with one slot for every space on the disk where data can be stored. When a file is modified, DOS marks the map accordingly. The directory entry points to the map, the map points to the disk.

The second thing DOS does when you ERASE or DELete a file is clear the FAT entries for that file—that is, it clears a portion of the map. It doesn't clear the data from the disk, because that would be a waste of time. It merely indicates to itself that when another file needs space on the disk, this area is available to be rewritten. Likewise, when a new directory entry is created, DOS will write over the first entry it finds marked with a sigma. It's worth emphasizing: until DOS rewrites the disk, the data is still there. Even if the deleted reference no longer shows when UnErasing or Undeleting, it is possible a directory slot was re-used but that the actual file information has not been overwritten.

It is especially true under DOS major Version 3.x that data shouldn't be considered totally lost until a low-level search has been made of the disk. DOS 3.x has a peculiar way of allocating disk space. Whenever a file is created or copied, DOS 3.x looks for an empty space big enough to hold it. The next time this happens, it looks farther out the disk. This process continues as long as you don't reboot or turn the power off, DOS looking through the FAT farther and farther away from the start of the disk for free space. The implication here is that after you've deleted a file, DOS doesn't necessarily use that area of the disk the next time it writes something to the disk. Odds are, in fact, that it won't (unlike DOS major Version 2.x, where odds are it will.)

Recovery is detailed on page   110.

Chapter 2
Recovery

Problems

This section covers most common failures, such as accidental erasure or format, and a few uncommon ones, such as invalid subdirectories. In almost all cases, you can still get a DOS prompt, but have troubles beyond there, either reading the disk, performing DOS operations such as copying, entering subdirectories, locating a file, and executing it. In a sense, all these errors are a result of some flaw or damage in the DOS file structure.

Recovery procedures are categorized according to the DOS error messages you would normally receive. It's always possible the error is due to faulty hardware. I have organized the book diagnostically, so that where more than one possibility exists you are urged simply to move to the next procedure. I'll tell you when and if it looks like a hardware problem and where to go for help.

It's always wise to reboot the machine with a DOS system diskette in A: before recovering. This eliminates any possible conflicts with resident software or device drivers, which often contributed to the original disaster. If you use the original DOS diskette to boot, immediately FORMAT a blank diskette with the /s (system) option. Then put the original DOS diskette back in a safe place.

"Abort, Retry, Ignore?" or "Abort, Retry, Fail?" Message From DOS

DIAGNOSIS: The format information for a sector has been clobbered or has gone bad. This may be a defect showing up on the disk, or it may be caused by software gone momentarily haywire and scrambling the disk. Anything from stray dogs kicking the power cable out to stray neutrinos can bring it on. No matter. The effect is the same: DOS can't read, write, or copy some area of the disk.

TOOLS REQUIRED: Mace Utilities Diagnose and Remedy.

KNOWLEDGE REQUIRED: Each sector of data on your disk is composed of two parts, the format information, and the data itself. While the data part is rewritten over and over, the format information is written only once. It has a strictly defined pattern that must not be altered.

What happens is one of a number of things. A program can go haywire, hardware can fail, the disk surface itself may wear out, or a latent defect makes its presence known. For more information read the sections on hard and floppy disks. The main point is either the format information is unreadable, which results in an Address mark or "sector not found" message, along with Abort, Retry. Or something has impermissibly altered the data since it was last recorded, which results in a CRC, or data error message just before the Abort, Retry message.

From a recovery viewpoint, it doesn't matter. You want to achieve two things: First, get the file into readable form with no (or minimum) data loss; second, lock-out the suspect area of this disk so it doesn't get used again by DOS. You don't want to go through this again. You can resolve the whole thing automatically with Mace Remedy and you can work around it with Norton's Disk Test.

Up to here I've assumed you are getting this message when you try to load a program or data file, or perform a DOS operation such as COPY. There is another, less pretty possibility, that the defect is in the system area of the disk, that is, where the Boot, File Allocation Tables, or Root Directory are located. You can confirm this is a problem by running Mace Diagnose or Mace Remedy or Norton's Disk Test. Curing it is another matter, which I'll go into below.

Knowledge Required

CURE: While there are a number of diagnostic tools such as Disk Test (DT) in the Norton Utilities that will tell you which spot and which file are affected, as of this writing only Mace Utilities Remedy will detect and lock-out automatically *and* fix the file at the same time. Remedy will, in fact, often retrieve data intact where repeated **Retry** fails. Where it can't fix the file, it'll move it to a safe place and put dummy information where the unrecoverable data went. This means the file can be read and quite often corrected. Loss is usually restricted to 512 bytes of data or less. It is certainly better to retype that small missing portion than it is to give up the entire file as lost because you can't copy it.

Cure

When the System Area Is Affected on a Hard Disk

The news isn't all that much better on a hard disk. Unlike data in files, the system area is dedicated; it can't be moved to a safe place. Worse, because this is a hard disk, you probably put files in subdirectories. That means you can UnFormat the disk with either Mace, Norton, or PC-Tools. But first you must Format the disk safely.

You can use Format-h from Mace Utilities to safely format any hard disk. Or you can safely use PC-DOS, or you can use any version of MS-DOS Format with the following exceptions: Compaq MS-DOS prior to Version 3.21, ATT MS-DOS prior to Version 3.1 Revision 1.01, and Burroughs MS-DOS. They are all lethal. They erase the disk! If you want to know more, read the section on FORMAT.

What we're hoping here is that the

disk wasn't damaged physically, or so badly defective that it can't hold a format for even a short while.

If you had Mace, Norton Advanced, or PC-Tools Deluxe installed, you can UnFormat and restore the backup information and you'll be in good shape. Read the sections on UnFormat.

If one of the big three weren't installed, Mace 5.0 Unformat will make the best of what it can find in the way of existing FAT and Directory information. You may recover none or all of your data. Backup, or copy everything that was recovered to another disk, and check each recovered file for integrity. Then start thinking very seriously about a new hard disk. At the very least, you should run an advanced diagnostic program, such as IBM's or HTEST, listed in the back of the book.

The critical system area must remain defect-free for safe operation. While DOS after Version 3.1 no longer lets you move the first partition up the disk, away from the defective area, XFdisk, which comes with HTest, will. That means you can create a DOS partition on the disk beyond where the defect is and save yourself several hundred dollars.

Cure

When the System Area Is Affected on a Floppy Disk

The news is not good. Unlike data in files, the system area is dedicated; it can't be moved to a safe place. Worse,

Cure

because this is a floppy, you probably don't put files in subdirectories, everything is in the root.

What you can do is Format the diskette with Mace Utilities Format-f using the /r option, for resurrect. Format-f will preserve all the readable data and lay down fresh format information. What we're hoping here is that the diskette wasn't damaged physically, or so badly defective that it can't hold a format for even a short while. Don't use DOS FORMAT on your floppy! It'll erase the diskette and recovery will be impossible.

Of course, Format-f may not be able to fix *and* restore the damaged area, so you'll need a second step: UnFormat the diskette with Mace 5.0 Unformat. The program will make the best of what it can find in the way of FAT and Directory information. You may recover none or all of your data. Copy everything that was recovered to another disk, and check each recovered file for integrity. Then discard the original, defective floppy; even if recovery was perfect, you don't want to chance using that diskette again.

"File *Something* Cross-Linked on Cluster N" Message From CHKDSK

Mace or PC-Tools Deluxe *was* installed.

DIAGNOSIS:

Some program has damaged the DOS file structure on your disk. Two files now point to the same data, or a single file is linked recursively to itself.

TOOLS REQUIRED:

Mace RXBAK or PC-Tools Deluxe MIRROR must have been installed.

KNOWLEDGE REQUIRED:

There is one entry in the FAT for every cluster of data on the disk. When a file is created or modified it's assigned one or more of those FAT entries for its exclusive use. Files can no more sensibly share FAT entries than you can share addresses with your neighbor. If they do, they are said to be *cross-linked*. Two files point to the same data. Or one file, instead of ending, points back to the middle of itself.

This situation is created by programs that manipulate the FAT or Directories: defraggers, directory sorters, disk sector editors, or sometimes just an ordinary program gone berserk. I don't mean to sound mystical. I know many of you think of these machines as stable and reliable; they are, and then again, they aren't. Things happen. From my perspective, it's a wonder things don't happen more often. I tend to focus on the cures more than the nature of the mysteries, which are only revealed over time.

CHKDSK won't cure cross-links. Neither will Norton. But both Mace and PC-Tools Deluxe allow a backup copy of the FATs, and can make use of it to restore files. If you haven't rebooted more than once since the cross-links were created, you may be able to recover intact.

Knowledge Required

CURE: First, note the names of the files CHKDSK reports as cross-linked. Usually they come in pairs. Copy them all to somewhere else on the disk. Make a special directory. Delete all the originals.

Run CHKDSK /F. The /F is essential; if you don't use it, CHKDSK merely goes through the motions and never actually corrects error. You may see a message "n lost clusters in n chains—convert to files, yes or no" Answer yes. These fragments may be valuable. They will be recovered to the root directory as FILE0000.CHK, FILE0001.CHK, etc.

UnDelete the cross-linked files with Mace or PC-Tools Deluxe. Check the recovered files for integrity.

If you rebooted after the cross-links were made, your MIRROR file will be useless and PC-Tools won't work.

Mace, however, keeps two generations of the FAT. You'll need to rename BACKUP.M_U to something else, then rename OLDBACK.M_U to BACKUP.M_U. This causes Mace UnDelete to use the next oldest copy of the FAT to find the proper FAT entries for the damaged files.

If recovery doesn't succeed, check the copies you made. Typically, one file of each cross-linked pair will be intact, the other corrupt. The corrupt files may simply be missing pieces at the end; if you converted lost clusters to .CHK files with CHKDSK /F, these files may contain the missing pieces. Try the DOS TYPE command to display them on the screen: TYPE filename and press RETURN.

You can concatenate, that is, chain the pieces back together with a little-known feature of the DOS COPY command. COPY file1/b + file2 newfile. This would put file1 and file2 together in newfile. Note the /b after file1. This tells DOS to make an exact splice. Otherwise it will treat the fragments as plain ASCII text and will no doubt fail to attach all the data. This process isn't destructive; you can try it over if the operation fails. Read the DOS manual for more, not necessarily more enlightening, information.

Cure

SUMMARY:

Cross-linked files result from mangling of the FAT or directory information. If Mace RXBAK was run, or PC-Tools Deluxe MIRROR, an older, accurate copy

Summary

of the FAT is available. Deleting the files and UnDeleting with Mace or PC-Tools Deluxe can often restore the accuracy of the FAT and integrity of the cross-linked files. When Norton inevitably catches up and begins making use of his backup file, you'll be able to do the same trick with his utilities.

"File *Something* Cross-Linked on Cluster N" Message From CHKDSK

Mace or PC-Tools Deluxe *wasn't* installed.

DIAGNOSIS:

Some program has damaged the DOS file structure on your disk. Two files now point to the same data, or a single file is linked recursively to itself.

TOOLS REQUIRED:

DOS CHKDSK.

KNOWLEDGE REQUIRED:

There is one entry in the FAT for every cluster of data on the disk. When a file is created or modified it's assigned one or more of those FAT entries for its exclusive use. Files can no more sensibly share FAT entries than you can share addresses with your neighbor. If they do, they are said to be *cross-linked*. Two files point to the same data. Or one file, instead of ending, points back to the middle of itself.

This situation is created by programs that manipulate the FAT or Directories: defraggers, directory sorters, disk sector editors, or sometimes it is just an ordinary program gone berserk. I don't mean to sound mystical. I know many of you think of these machines as stable and reliable; they are, and then again, they aren't. Things happen. From my perspective, it's a wonder things don't happen more often. I tend to focus on the cures more than the nature of the mysteries, which are only revealed over time.

CHKDSK won't cure cross-links. Neither will Norton. Both Mace and PC-Tools Deluxe allow a backup copy of the FATs, and can make use of it to restore files, but only when installed beforehand. You'll have to do it the hard way.

Knowledge Required

CURE: First, note the names of the files CHKDSK reports as cross-linked. Usually they come in pairs. Copy them all to somewhere else on the disk—or on a different disk. Make a special directory. Delete all the originals.

Run CHKDSK /F. The /F (Fix) option is essential; when you don't use it, CHKDSK never actually corrects errors, it just reports them. You may see a message "n lost clusters in n chains—convert to files, yes or no" Answer yes. These fragments may or may not be valuable. They will be recovered to the root directory as FILE0000.CHK, FILE0001.CHK, etc.

Now, check each of the copies you made for integrity. One file of each cross-linked pair will typically be intact, the other corrupt. The corrupt files will often be missing pieces at the end; if you converted lost clusters to .CHK files with CHKDSK /F, those files may contain the missing pieces.

Try the DOS TYPE command to display them on the screen: TYPE filename and press RETURN.

You can concatenate, that is, chain the pieces back together with a little-known feature of the DOS COPY command. COPY file1/b + file2 newfile. This would put file1 and file2 together in newfile. Note the /b after file1. This tells DOS to make an exact splice on this and all other pieces. Otherwise it will treat the fragments as plain ASCII text and will no doubt fail to attach all the data. This process isn't destructive; you can try it over. If the operation fails, read the DOS manual for more information.

Cure

SUMMARY:

Cross-linked files result from mangling of the FAT or directory information. If Mace RXBAK was run, or PC-Tools Deluxe MIRROR, an older, accurate copy of the FAT is available, making recovery more certain. Otherwise, copying the files and deleting the originals will cure the cross-links. But, typically, at best one in two of the copied files will be intact.

"*N* Lost Clusters Found in *N* Chains—Convert to Files, Yes or No" Message From CHKDSK

DIAGNOSIS:

Some program has stranded data on the disk without creating a directory entry. If no other error messages are encountered, this is no cause for concern. If other errors were reported, the .CHK files may be very important. Look-up and read the sections on "Invalid subdirectory", "Invalid start address", "Invalid size—file truncated", and "Cross-linked files".

TOOLS REQUIRED:

DOS CHKDSK.

KNOWLEDGE REQUIRED:

When space is allocated to a file, the corresponding address in the File Allocation Table is filled out and, ordinarily, a directory entry is created that points to that FAT entry. If the Directory entry is damaged, or never created—it happens, usually with programs written for older versions of DOS, or when you break out of a program by rebooting or turning off the power without first exiting to the DOS prompt—the FAT entry is stranded. Space is allocated, but no one claims it or the data stored there. CHKDSK

Knowledge Required

wants you to either let it free up the space for storage, or create a directory entry for it.

CURE: Run CHKDSK /F. Note the /F. If you don't use it, CHKDSK merely goes through the motions of recovery; it does not actually fix anything.

". . . convert to files, yes . . ."

Answering yes will cause CHKDSK to create a directory entry in the root of the drive being checked, one for every lost chain. These files will show up as FILE0000.CHK, FILE0001.CHK, etc.

Use the DOS TYPE command to display the .CHK files on your screen, and try to make sense of them. Files that begin with Mz are .EXE programs (Mz stands for Mark Zibikowski, one of the architects of DOS) and you can usually get fresh copies from the original disk.

Bear in mind, in the absence of other errors, these are most likely temporary files created by an application for its own use. They may look like important data, so check the file you think that information should be in. If it looks intact then the .CHK file is probably just scratchpad information, and can be safely deleted.

If other errors were reported, the .CHK files may be very important. Look-up and read the sections on "Invalid subdirectory" and "Cross-linked files".

Cure

"... convert to files, no ..."

If no other errors were reported along with "... lost clusters," you can say **no** and CHKDSK /F will simply delete the FAT entries, freeing up the space for future storage. It will report how much disk space was freed.

SUMMARY:

Lost clusters represent data stranded on the disk with no directory entry. Usually these are temporary files— scratchpad information—used by some application. In the absence of other error messages, you can say "no" to converting them to files, and free up the disk space for new data. If in doubt, you can say "yes" and examine the .CHK files CHKDSK creates for valuable data. If other errors are reported, always say "yes".

You can often avoid this situation by exiting programs in an orderly manner, rather than just switching off the machine, or pressing Ctrl-Alt-Del to escape.

"Invalid Subdirectory" Message Reported by CHKDSK or DOS

DIAGNOSIS:

If DOS gave you the alert, you may have typed the name wrong. If you don't think that's the case, run CHKDSK. It should report the same thing. If not, you either have a spelling error, or the directory no longer exists.

If you don't get a corresponding "convert to file?" request, this simply means either the . or .. reference at the head of the subdirectory has been corrupted. This is not particularly serious.

Run CHKDSK /V (for Verbose) and you should see, as it runs through all the files, a message like ". entry has a bad link . . . attribute . . . size."

If you did get a "convert to file" request, skip to the next recovery section: "Invalid subdirectory—convert to file . . ."

TOOLS REQUIRED:

DOS major Version 3.x and CHKDSK.COM or CHKDSK.EXE.

KNOWLEDGE REQUIRED:

When you do a DIRectory of a subdirectory, the first two entries you see are . and .. They have meaning. . refers to the subdirectory itself, while .. refers to the directory it branches from.

Knowledge Required

(As the root directory doesn't branch from any other, it has no . or .. reference).

You can in fact CD to .. and DOS will take you to the directory where the current one appears listed. You can even COPY . to .. and all the files in the current directory will be copied to its parent. When the directory entries for . or .. are corrupted, typically by a directory sort program, defragger, or use of a disk sector editor, CHKDSK reports an error.

Operations aren't affected. DOS can work around the problem. But the file structure of the disk isn't, strictly speaking, intact.

CURE: Under DOS major Version 3.x you can cure this problem by running **CHKDSK /F**. Note, the **/F** (for Fix) is crucial, otherwise CHKDSK merely goes through the motions and never actually writes any changes to disk.

Even if you normally run under DOS major Version 2.x and don't, for some reason, wish to convert, you can boot once with a DOS 3 system floppy and use its version of CHKDSK to cure the problem. Or, you can live with it.

SUMMARY: In the absence of other errors, an "invalid subdirectory" message signifies damage to the . or .. entries at the head of a subdirectory. DOS can live

Summary

with this; if you can too, do nothing.
Otherwise, when booted under DOS
major Version 3.x and using its
CHKDSK /F, you can fix the problem
and make the error message go away.

"Invalid Subdirectory— Convert to File, Yes or No"

Recovery with Mace.

DIAGNOSIS: Something has damaged the directory entry, and it no longer points to directory information. Or something has damaged the directory information itself. Rarely, something put junk into a directory, which DOS tries to interpret as a directory reference.

  If this was a valid directory, you should also see a "xxx Lost cluster in yyy chains" report when you run CHKDSK.

TOOLS REQUIRED: In addition to DOS CHKDSK, you may need the Mace Utilities Sector Editor.

KNOWLEDGE REQUIRED: Read the section of this manual titled Disk Sector Editors.

  Other than the root, directories are files just like any other file, except that they contain directory entries as data and the first two entries must be named . and .. If DOS can't find . and .. in the first two entries, it'll reject the directory, even if everything else is good information.

  Recovery depends on what, exactly, caused the screw-up. If something damaged the File Allocation Table,

DOS may not be able to find that actual directory information on the disk. Depending on the extent of the FAT damage, this may be corrected with a disk sector editor. I should say, perfect recovery is possible, but it depends on your patience and skill—mostly your patience.

Knowledge Required

If it was a directory sort gone haywire, recovery could be as simple as fixing the first two entry names with a sector editor. If the DIR command shows a piece of nonsense as a directory, you'll need a sector editor to get rid of it.

QUICK CURE:

If CHKDSK reports "n lost clusters in n chains—convert to files . . ." you can be reasonably certain that those chains of data are the files that were stored in the damaged subdirectory. If you say "yes" they'll be converted to .CHK files in the root of the drive being checked.

The good news is you've recovered them; the bad news is they're now named FILE0000.CHK, FILE0001.CHK, etc. You'll have to figure out which is which, based on size, or by examining them with an editor or the DOS TYPE command. There is also a small problem with size; CHKDSK recovers the files in round clusters. That means all or most will have some extra junk tacked on to the end. While some programs know where the true End-of-File is, many rely on the file size as shown by DOS, and this is now incorrect. Text files are rela-

Quick Cure

tively easy to fix; program files can be reloaded from the originals. Others you will have to experiment with.

If there are hundreds of lost chains, you might have a problem—the root normally holds only 512 total files. CHKDSK will abort, you'll have to copy the .CHK files to some other disk or disks, delete them, and run CHKDSK /F again to recover more. This is a classic situation where hurrying the recovery process, either to satisfy your anxieties or your love of action and quick results, can lead you to spend more time in the long run than you would with a more patient approach.

CURE: *With Mace MUSE*

Version 5.0 of the Mace Utilities contains a sector editor, MUSE, which will allow you to correct the error. The most straightforward way to approach this is to change to the directory where the affected directory is listed when you do a DIR.

Type MUSE and press RETURN. You will see what looks like a normal directory listing in the midst of other information. The difference with this listing is the cursor. You can edit it.

Most importantly, the Ins and Del keys operate as cut-and-paste when looking at a directory. That is, press Alt-Del and the entry under the cursor will be deleted to a clipboard; press Alt-Ins and it will be copied to the line under the cursor. If nothing is on the clipboard, a blank entry will be inserted.

First, move the cursor to the entry we're concerned about. Does it show as a directory? If not, we'll have to correct its *attribute*.

Press the Tab key until it hops to the directory attribute column. Press the number "1." ESCape to DOS and run CHKDSK. All may or may not be well.

If you still get errors, type MUSE again, move the cursor to the directory entry that concerns us, press RETURN and continue reading.

Use PgUp and PgDn to look for the . and .. entries. They may be there, but simply shuffled out of place. If you see them, use the Alt-Del key to clip them out one at time, then PgUp and Alt-Ins to paste them in first and second. When you're done, ESCape to DOS and try CHKDSK again. All should be well now.

. and .. may be missing entirely. With the cursor on the first line, press Alt-Ins twice, and two blank directory entries will be inserted. Press the . key, and MUSE will fill out the first line as best it can. Move the cursor down to the second line and press the . key twice. MUSE will fill out the .. entry as best it can. Now ESCape to DOS and try CHKDSK again. All should be well.

To get rid of a directory that points to something other than directory information, you can run CHKDSK /F and answer the ". . . convert to file"

Cure

Cure

query with a "yes." This changes the attribute on the file to "normal."

Alternately, you can enter MUSE as we did at first, from the directory where you see the listing for the directory that concerns us. Position the cursor on that entry, press Del, and ESCape to DOS. Run CHKDSK, and all should be well, with the possibility that lost cluster will be reported. Run CHKDSK /F (for Fix) and answer "yes" convert to files, if you're interested at all in files that used to be in that directory. Otherwise answer "no" and the disk space will be freed.

To fix a directory that currently points to something other than directory information, enter MUSE as we did at first, from the directory where you see the listing for the directory that concerns us. Position the cursor on that entry and press TAB until the cursor hops to the "Start Address" column. This is where the directory currently points in the File Allocation Table and disk, and it is wrong.

We need to find the right place on the disk. Select "Search" and enter a search pattern. If you know the name of one of the first 14 files that used to appear in this directory, enter that name. Otherwise enter a period followed by seven spaces, then press RETURN. MUSE will search the entire disk, if necessary, for a match and show you what it found. More importantly, it shows where it found it. Continue the search until you find what looks like the start of the missing directory entries. Fear not, you'll know them when you see them. Note the cluster number, ESCape from the search, and enter that number in the "Start Address" column. This may be only the first step, but let's see how far we've come.

ESCape to DOS and change directories to the one we just worked on. Do a DIR. Anything there? If it's all there, try CHKDSK. If all's well, congratulations. If the directory looked good, but CHKDSK showed it as being cross-linked, it would be a good idea to copy your files off, or back them up, then remove the directory with MUSE and clean up lost clusters with CHKDSK / F.

Cure

If the directory was incomplete, we have some work to do on the File Allocation Table. We will need to locate all the pieces of the directory and connect them in a FAT chain. MUSE automates this process. Still, patience . . .

Back into MUSE again, place cursor on the first line of the bad directory, and press Alt-J for jump. You should be looking at the directory data located by Searching. Now select FILE view with the appropriate key—this is the same stuff, only not formatted to look like a directory. This is how things actually look on your disk, cryptic, but still identifiable as directory information. Now select FAT. This shows you the File Allocation Table for that area of the disk, with the current cluster highlighted. Again, press the function key for FILE view, and you'll see we

Cure

switched back. Get the idea? FAT view shows the FAT entry for the data you're looking at in FILE view.

Select FAT view again and let's look at the possibilities. The best luck is an entry under the cursor that shows empty—the FAT entry contains a 0. Select "Chain" mode, and use the right arrow key to move to the next unallocated cluster in the FAT. Select "FILE" to view it. We're looking for more of the directory. You can also Search if you know a filename to look for. When you find what you want, either way, select FAT view again. When Chain is selected, every time you press return, the current cluster is added to the file and the FAT is filled out appropriately. When you're done, you can press ESCape to return to DOS. All should be well, or at least considerably improved.

The worst case would be where MUSE helped you Search out the directory pieces you wanted, but showed that they were already allocated to some other file, one that wasn't a directory.

The Recovery procedure is similar to the one above, except that you'll break the link between your directory information and the file that's claiming it, then Chain will attach it to the directory we're trying to build. Bear in mind, if this is the case, your disk or FATs or both may have been substantially scrambled. You will not only need to fix the directory itself, but other files.

Back into MUSE again, place the

cursor on the bad directory. You should
be looking at the directory data located
by Searching. Now select FILE view
with the appropriate function key—
this is the same stuff, only not formatted to look like a directory. This is how
things actually look on your disk, cryptic, but still identifiable as directory information. Now select FAT view with
the appropriate function key. This
shows you the File Allocation Table for
that area of the disk, with the current
cluster highlighted. Again, press the
function key for FILE view, and you'll
see we switched back. Get the idea?
FAT view shows the FAT entry for the
data you're looking at in FILE view.

Cure

Select FAT view again. The entry
under the cursor shows something
other than empty. It could be End-of-
File, or the number of some other place
in the FAT. MUSE shows you who it
belongs to. If it's not our directory, or
shows cross-linking, you can break the
connection by pressing Del (the delete
key). Press RETURN and you can reconnect it to the directory only. Now,
select Chain mode, press RETURN and
use PgDn, or Search if you know a filename to look for, to look the disk over
for the next piece of directory. When
you find what you want, either way, select FAT view again and repeat the
earlier process. If the entry is empty
(zero) you can simply press RETURN.
Otherwise break the link with Del.

When Chain is selected, every time
you press return, the current cluster is
added to the file and the FAT is filled

Cure

out appropriately. You're building a legitimate file out of material sorted on the disk. When you're done, you can press ESCape to return to DOS. All should be well, or at least considerably improved.

SUMMARY:

Damaged directories can often be repaired by correcting or recreating the . and .. entries. More extensive damage can be repaired with MUSE in a straightforward manner. Though it still requires some patience, recovery with MUSE doesn't require a high level of computer sophistication.

"Invalid Subdirectory— Convert to File, Yes or No"

Recovery with Norton.

DIAGNOSIS:

Something has damaged the directory entry, and it no longer points to directory information. Or something has damaged the directory information itself. Rarely, something put junk into a directory, which DOS tries to interpret as a directory reference.

If this was a valid directory, you should also see a "*n* Lost cluster in *n* chains" report when you run CHKDSK.

TOOLS REQUIRED:

In addition to DOS CHKDSK, you may need the Norton 4.0 or Norton Advanced.

KNOWLEDGE REQUIRED:

Other than the root, directories are files just like any other file, except that they contain directory entries as data and the first two entries must be named . and .. If DOS can't find . and .. in the first two entries, it'll reject the directory, even if everything else is good information.

Recovery depends on what, exactly, caused the screw-up. If something damaged the File Allocation Table, DOS may not be able to find that actual directory information on the disk. Depending on the extent of the FAT damage, this may be corrected with a disk sector editor. I should say, perfect recovery is possible, but it depends on your patience and skill—mostly your patience.

If it was a directory sort gone haywire, recovery could be as simple as fixing the first two entry names with a sector editor. If the DIR command shows a piece of nonsense as a directory, you'll need a sector editor to get rid of it.

Knowledge Required

QUICK CURE: If CHKDSK reports "*n* lost clusters in *n* chains—convert to files . . ." you can be reasonably certain that those chains of data are the files that were stored in the damaged subdirectory. If you say "yes" they'll be converted to .CHK files in the root of the drive being checked.

The good news is you've recovered them; the bad news is they're now named FILE0000.CHK, FILE0001.CHK, etc. You'll have to figure out which is which based on size, or by examining them with an editor or the DOS TYPE command. There is also a small problem with size; CHKDSK recovers the files in round clusters. That means all or most will have some extra junk tacked onto the end. While some programs know where the true End-of-File is, many rely on the file size as shown by DOS, and this is now incorrect. Text files are relatively easy to fix; program files can be reloaded from the originals. Others you will have to experiment with.

If there are hundreds of lost chains, you might have a problem—the root normally holds only 512 total files. CHKDSK will abort. You'll have to copy the .CHK files to some other disk or disks, delete them, and run CHKDSK /F again to recover more.

This is a classic situation where hurrying the recovery process, either to satisfy your anxieties, or your love of action and quick results, can lead you to spend more time in the long run than you would with a more patient approach.

Quick Cure

CURE: Version 4.0 of the Norton Utilities contains a sector editor built into NU, which will allow you to correct some errors.

The most straightforward way to approach this is to change to the directory where the affected directory is listed when you do a DIR.

Type **NU** (or **NORTON**) and press RETURN.

Press RETURN to select the default (Explore Disk).

Press RETURN again to select default (Choose Item).

Press RETURN again to select default (File).

If you started in the root directory,

because your damaged directory branched from there, press RETURN again to select default (Root dir).

If you started in a subdirectory, use the arrow keys to position the highlight bar on the . entry (current directory) and press RETURN.

You'll see what looks something like a normal directory listing, with additional information. The difference with this listing is the cursor. You can edit it.

First, move the cursor to the entry we're concerned about. Does it show as a directory? You should see a DIR in the "DIR" column on the far right, opposite the directory name. If not, we'll have to correct its *attribute*.

Cure

Press the Tab key until it hops to the attribute DIR column. Press any key and a DIR should appear. You can arrow or shift-tab back and try again—attributes simply toggle on and off when you touch a key. Normally a directory will have only the DIR attribute set; if others are on, note which ones, then turn them all off except DIR.

Press ESCape and Norton will ask if you want to write corrections—press "w" for write. Then ESCape to DOS and run CHKDSK. All may or may not be well.

If you still get errors, type NU again. Take the defaults again to get to the damaged entry. This time we'll go one step further in the select File menu. We'll position the highlight bar on the directory name itself, rather than Root or . and press RETURN. Press E for Edit.

. and .. may simply be shuffled out of place. Use PgUp and PgDn to look for the . and ..entries. If you see them, write down the information for both: date, time, start, attribute. For entries that branch from the root, .. will have a blank start number.

Next, we have to mark each one as deleted. To do that, position the cursor on the first character of the . directory name. Press **F2** for Hex display. This shows data as it looks on the disk. Type E and **5**, and note in the right column how the first character, ., of the directory name has changed to a sigma. As far as DOS is concerned the entry is

Cure

now deleted.

Press F4 to get DIR view and move the highlight bar to the .. entry. Position the cursor on the first period in the name and press F2. Again type E and **5**, and note the sigma at the right. DOS now treats the entry as deleted.

You are a third of the way home. Next, you need to PgUp to the start of the directory. Take a look at what's there, where . and .. should be; you'll need to move the first two entries. (I am assuming you're not in the root directory and these are not IBMBIO.COM and IBMDOS.COM, or IO.SYS and MSDOS.SYS. If they are, start over.)

Copy the information for the first two entries, or use Shift-PrtSc to print them out. You'll have to re-create them in the slots where you deleted the old . and .. entries.

Next, you want to type in the information for . and .. in the first two slots. That is, on the first line type a period, then seven spaces, then three more spaces, a zero for size, then the date, and time you wrote down. Now clear all attributes except DIR. Position the cursor with TAB and press any key to toggle the attribute on and off. Do the same on the second line for .. Make sure you add spaces after the . and .. to erase anything else that was there.

Press ESCape and Norton will ask if you want to write corrections. Press "w" for write. Then ESCape to DOS and run CHKDSK. All may or may not be well.

Cure

If the two files that were in first and second place weren't critical, forget them. They are deleted, though CHKDSK /F will probably be necessary top delete the chains of space allocated to them. Answer no to the "convert to files" message. Or you can answer yes and retrieve and rename them. Or you can go back into NU and manually enter them in the slots where we deleted the misplaced . and .. entries.

The procedure for recreating the two missing entries is the same as for placing a new . and .. in the first two slots.

To get rid of a directory that points to something other than directory information, enter NU as we did at first, from the directory where you see the listing for the directory that concerns us. Position the cursor on the first character in that entry, press **F2** for Hex view, then press E and **5**. ESCape to DOS (answer "w" when Norton asks permission to write). Run CHKDSK, and all should be well, with the possibility that lost cluster will be reported. Run CHKDSK /F (for Fix) and answer "yes" convert to files, if you are interested at all in files that used to be in that directory. Otherwise answer "no" and the disk space will be freed.

. and .. may be missing entirely. While it's theoretically possible to recover from this or worse conditions with Norton, it would take more understanding and experience than a single book could impart. Simpler to get Mace and read the section using MUSE to recover.

To fix a directory that currently points to something other than directory information, again, better to get Mace and read the section on using MUSE.

If the directory was incomplete, we have some work to do on the File Allocation Table. We'll need to locate all the pieces of the directory and connect them in a FAT chain. Again, Mace MUSE automates this process.

Cure

SUMMARY: A fair number of directory problems relate to damage to the . and .. entries. Some of these problems can be corrected by ordinary users with the cur-

Summary

rent version of Norton's disk sector editor. Some can't, unless you are already a bit of a wizard. Even then, the wise thing to do would be to get and use Mace, because it's easier and saves time.

"Invalid Subdirectory— Convert to File, Yes or No"

Recovery with PC-Tools.

DIAGNOSIS:

Something has damaged the directory entry, and it no longer points to directory information. Or something has damaged the directory information itself. Rarely, something put junk into a directory, which DOS tries to interpret as a directory reference.

If this was a valid directory, you should also see a "*n* lost cluster in *n* chains" report when you run CHKDSK.

TOOLS REQUIRED:

In addition to DOS CHKDSK, you may need PC-Tools.

KNOWLEDGE REQUIRED:

Other than the root, directories are files just like any other file, except that they contain directory entries as data and the first two entries must be named . and .. If DOS can't find . and .. in the first two entries, it'll reject the directory, even if everything else is good information.

Recovery depends on what, exactly, caused the screw-up. If something damaged the File Allocation Table, DOS may not be able to find that actual directory information on the disk.

Depending on the extent of the FAT damage, this may be corrected with a disk sector editor. I should say, perfect recovery is possible, but it depends on your patience and skill—mostly your patience.

If it was a directory sort gone haywire, recovery could be as simple as fixing the first two entry names with a sector editor. If the DIR command shows a piece of nonsense as a directory, you'll need a sector editor to get rid of it.

Knowledge Required

QUICK CURE: If CHKDSK reports "*n* lost clusters in *n* chains—convert to files . . ." you can be reasonably certain that those chains of data are the files that were stored in the damaged subdirectory. If you say "yes" they'll be converted to .CHK files in the root of the drive being checked.

The good news is you've recovered them; the bad news is they're now named FILE0000.CHK, FILE0001.CHK, etc. You'll have to figure out which is which, based on size, or by examining them with an editor or the DOS TYPE command. There is also a small problem with size; CHKDSK recovers the files in round clusters. That means all or most will have some extra junk tacked onto the end. While some programs know where the true End-of-File is, many rely on the file size as shown by DOS, and this is now incorrect. Text files are relatively easy to fix; program files can be reloaded from the originals. Others you will have to experiment with.

If there are hundreds of lost chains, you might have a problem—the root normally holds only 512 total files. CHKDSK will abort. You'll have to copy the .CHK files to some other disk or disks, delete them, and run CHKDSK /F again to recover more.

This is a classic situation where hurrying the recovery process, either to satisfy your anxieties, or your love of action and quick results, can lead you to spend more time in the long run than you would with a more patient approach.

Quick Cure

CURE: PC-Tools contains a built-in sector editor that will allow you correct some errors. It's not my favorite. Norton makes this much easier, Mace easiest of all. But it can be done.

Type **PCTOOLS** and press RETURN.

Press **F3** to select the alternate menu. PC-Tools will request a drive letter. Supply one.

Press **M** for Map. PC-Tools will request a drive letter again. Supply one.

Press **F** for files.

Press **F10** to select a new directory. Use the PgUp and Pgdn and the up and down arrows to hi-light the dam-

Cure

aged directory. Press **G** for Go to select it.

You'll return to the map. Press the left arrow. You should see a "D" appear on the map. At the top of the screen are two numbers, **Start cluster** is the one we're interested in. This is the starting cluster address of the damaged directory. Write it down. Then press EScape. If the damaged directory doesn't branch from the root directory, you'll have to repeat the last procedure. Press **F** again, then **F10** again and select the parent directory for the damaged one, that is, the one the damaged directory branches from. Once it is highlighted, press **G** for Go and left arrow. Write down the starting cluster number. It should be different from the previous number. If not, start over and go more slowly.

Remember, subdirectories are files just like any other file. They can be located anywhere on the disk and they can be fragmented. For every directory except the root there is a directory entry that points to the starting address of data stored somewhere else on the disk, and whose special attribute is "directory". This tells DOS that what it points to is more directory information.

You should be back at the first menu.

Press **E** for Edit.

Press **F2** to change sector number.

If your damaged directory branched

from the root, press **R** for Root. Otherwise enter the starting cluster for the directory it branched *from*.

Don't get confused. We're concerned with two distinct places here: the directory where your directory is listed (when you do a DIR command), known as the "parent," and the damaged directory itself, which shows your files. We want to check the parent first, to see if its listing is the thing that's damaged.

On the right-hand side of the screen you'll see what looks vaguely like a normal directory listing, the names and extensions followed by crazy characters. Move the cursor with the arrow keys and PgDn to the entry we're concerned about.

Cure

The first character after the filename (and extension, if any) should be a blunt right-pointing arrowhead. Don't worry about spaces. Press F3 for Edit.

To simply get rid of a directory that points to something other than directory information, press **E** and **5**. Note in the right-hand column how the first character of the filename changed to a sigma. Press **F5** to update the disk. ESCape to DOS and run CHKDSK, and all should be well, with the possibility that lost clusters will be reported. Run CHKDSK /F (for Fix) and answer "yes" convert to files, if you're interested at all in files that used to be in that directory. Otherwise answer "no" and the disk space will be freed.

To attempt to correct the problem, press **F1** to swap fields. The blinking

Cure

cursor will hop to the text column on the right.

Press the right arrow 11 times. (8 for the maximum filename, 3 for the maximum extension. You can see where those arbitrary limits come from; that is all the space allotted to them in the directory entry.) The cursor should be over a right-pointing arrowhead.

Press **F1** and the blinking cursor will hop back into that field of numbers that hogs the left two-thirds of the screen. It should be blinking on the twelfth pair of numbers on that line, the "1" of a pair "10."

Press **F1** several times to assure yourself you've got the twelfth character and twelfth pair. You might even take some time and find a good directory entry and play this game with it, to assure yourself you know what to look for. If the number is not 10, then correct it by typing 10. You should see an arrowhead appear over in the right column as soon as you finish typing the 0.

Press F5 to update. This will correct the entry on the disk. DOS will now try to interpret the information it points to as "directory information."

Press **ESC**ape twice and exit to DOS, and run CHKDSK. All may or may not be well.

If you still get errors, type PCTOOLS and press RETURN.

Press **F3**

Press **E** for Edit

Press F2 to change sector number

Press C for cluster, and enter the first number you copied, the starting cluster of the actual damaged directory itself. Press RETURN.

You're now back in the edit screen looking at the place where all the files associated with that directory are listed. Normally the first two entries would be . and ...

The problem might be that . and .. have been shuffled out of place. Use PgUp and PgDn to look for the . and .. entries. If you see them, print the screen, or write down the information for both. Each entry takes up two lines; that's thirty-two pairs of numbers each. Forget the characters in the right-hand column and concentrate on the left.

Having copied the information, next we have to mark each one as deleted. To do that, position the cursor on the first character of the first number pair for the . directory name. It should be "2E." We want it to read E5, so type "E" and "5" and note in the right column how the first character, ., of the directory name has changed to a sigma. As far as DOS is concerned the entry is now deleted.

Press the left arrow twice to get back to the start of the line, then down arrow twice. You should be on the 2E corresponding to the .. entry. If not, find it. Again type "E" and "5", and note the sigma at the right. DOS now treats the entry as deleted.

Cure

You are a third of the way home. Next, you need to PgUp to the start of the directory. Take a look at what's there, where . and .. should be; you'll need to move the first two entries. (I am assuming you're not in the root directory and these aren't IBMBIO.COM and IBMDOS.COM, or IO.SYS and MSDOS.SYS. If they are, start over.)

Copy the information for the first two entries, or use Shift-PrtSc to print them out. You will have to recreate them in the slots where you deleted the old . and .. entries.

Right now, you want to type in the information you copied for . and .. into the first two slots. That is, on the first line begin typing the letter pairs for . and keep typing. It should take exactly two lines. The information for .. will start on the third line and, again, take two lines.

Cure

Press F5 for Update. Press ESCape twice, exit to DOS, and run CHKDSK. All may or may not be well.

If the two files that were in first and second place weren't critical, forget them. They are deleted, though CHKDSK /F will probably be necessary to delete the chains of space allocated to them. Answer no, to the "convert to files" message. Or you can answer yes and retrieve and rename them. Or you can go back into PCTOOLS and manually enter them into the slots where we deleted the misplaced . and .. entries. The procedure for recreating the two missing entries is the same as for placing a new . and .. in the first two slots.

. and .. may be missing entirely. While it's theoretically possible to recover from this or worse conditions with PC-Tools, it would take more understanding and experience than a single book could impart. It would be simpler to get Mace and read the section using MUSE to recover.

Cure

To fix a directory that currently points to something other than directory information, again, better to get Mace and read the section on using MUSE.

If the directory was incomplete, we have some work to do on the File Allocation Table. We will need to locate all the pieces of the directory and connect them in a FAT chain. Again, Mace MUSE automates this process.

SUMMARY:

A fair number of directory problems relate to damage to the . and .. entries. Some of these problems can be corrected by ordinary users with the current version of PC-Tools disk sector editor. Some can't, unless you are already a bit of a wizard. Even then, the wise thing to do would be to use Mace, because it's easier and saves time.

"First Cluster Number Is Invalid, Entry Truncated" Message From CHKDSK

DIAGNOSIS:

Something has damaged the directory entry for that file. It no longer points to a valid entry in the File Allocation Table. Usually, the culprit is a program that has the power to muck about with your directories, such as directory sort, a defragger, or a disk sector editor. Disk caching software, or partitioning software that breaks the 32 megabyte barrier might also be at fault. Or it might be faulty memory switch settings or turbo boards rising to haunt the system.

I say "at fault" in the sense that there is some conflict going on between this software and something else on your machine. Unless you can identify and resolve the conflict, you'll have to forego using the software that was the proximate cause of the damage.

TOOLS REQUIRED:

DOS CHKDSK, and possibly Mace, Norton, or PC-Tools disk sector editor.

KNOWLEDGE REQUIRED:

In addition to a file's name, size, and creation time and date, its directory entry contains an address where the file starts on the disk. Actually this ad-

Knowledge Required

dress is the first in a chain of addresses; the rest of the chain is in the File Allocation Table. This one indicates where to look in the FAT to pick up the front end of the chain. If something alters it to a value of less than 2 or greater than the total number of data clusters on that drive, you'll get this message from CHKDSK. In effect, the directory entry points to nonsense.

That doesn't necessarily mean the file is lost. Usually, when you see this message you get an accompanying warning, x lost clusters in x chains— convert to files? This means that CHKDSK recognizes data space allocated on the disk for which there is no corresponding directory entry.

CURE: If you are lucky, there will be one invalid directory and one lost chain.

Type **CHKDSK /F** and press RETURN.

The **/F** is for "Fix". The lost chain will be converted to a file in the root directory and assigned the name FILE0000.CHK. Your original file will be assigned a length of zero.

COPY FILE0000.CHK to damaged filename and all should be well. CHKDSK should report a clean bill of health for the disk.

If more than one file was listed as having an invalid start address, you follow the same procedure, but CHKDSK /F will create a number of .CHK files. You will have to determine

Cure

which >CHK file goes with which damaged file. The fastest way is as follows:

On the command line, type TYPE FILE0000.CHK and press RETURN. If the first two characters are **Mz**, this is a .EXE program file. Delete it. You can, presumably, get fresh copies of executable programs from original disks.

All else depends on your ability to recognize something familiar in the data as it scrolls up the screen. If it's all Greek and beeps, you may have to look at the .CHK files with a sector editor from Mace, Norton, or PC-Tools. These will let you page through the files, no matter what the contents. Often you'll find embedded copyright messages that identify what program this is, or format information that helps identify what program created them.

Make notes as you go through all the .CHK files, then copy them to the respective damaged filenames. Don't delete the .CHK files until you're satisfied that all the damaged files that concern you are recovered and either run or load and are completely intact.

If this approach doesn't work, it probably means the File Allocation Table has also been damaged. If you haven't rebooted the machine since the damage was done, you can, if Mace, Norton, or PC-Tools was installed, restore the backup file. Before doing that, copy or backup any valuable files that aren't damaged, as restoring the backup may alter some good files.

The idea here is to restore an older and, hopefully, more accurate copy of the FAT and root directory. This is most effective when the damage is confined to the root directory on a hard disk. Recovery in that case may be near perfect. If, however, the damaged files were in subdirectories, you're only halfway home. Restoring the backup

Cure

doesn't cure subdirectories, which are simply files stored elsewhere on the disk. It does, however, give you an earlier copy of the FAT. CHKDSK should now report a more accurate set of lost clusters in lost chains. Go back to the start of this recovery section and begin again.

SUMMARY: If a directory entry is corrupted, commonly the address of where the file starts on the disk is set to an invalid number. Correcting this number with a sector editor isn't usually productive. This catastrophe, however, usually results in lost clusters in lost chains, which CHKDSK will reclaim. These files can then be examined and reassigned their original names.

"Probable Non-DOS Disk" on a Floppy Disk

DIAGNOSIS:

Floppy disk wasn't formatted with DOS.

TOOLS REQUIRED:

Mace Utilities program NONDOS, or a disk sector editor such as Norton or PC-Tools.

KNOWLEDGE REQUIRED:

The first value in the File Allocation Table on any valid DOS media is the Media Descriptor Byte. For fixed disks, this is defined as follows:

FE	160K, single-sided diskette
FF	320K, double-sided diskette
FC	180K, single-sided diskette
FD	360K, double-sided diskette
F9	720k, 1.2M or 1.44M diskette
F8	fixed disk
F0	other

If something other than a correct value is placed there, CHKDSK will complain. If that's all that's wrong, you can continue to run with no problems. Changing the value back to F8 will shut CHKDSK up.

The concern here is that something overwrote a part of the disk that should never be touched except by

FDISK or FORMAT. When this happens, you should think about what you've been running on your machine lately, any recent additions to your program library. That new program may not be solely to blame. Quite possibly there is some conflict with resident software or with device drivers declared in your CONFIG.SYS file.

Something, for sure, is not right. Next time the damage might be more extensive. Better to isolate the cause now, but first, back up all your data to floppies or some other drive.

Knowledge Required

CURE: You could, of course, always reformat the disk with DOS, if you don't mind backing up and restoring all your files.

With Mace

Mace contains a program, NONDOS, that lets you automatically reset the media descriptor to its proper value. Hard disks are virtually always F8.

With Norton 4.0

Type NU drive (or NORTON drive) and press RETURN. For example NU C: will bring the program up on the C: drive.

Press RETURN (selects default Explore Disk).

Press RETURN (selects next default, Choose Item).

Press RETURN (selects default, File).

Press up arrow, then RETURN (selects FAT Area).

Press E for Edit.

You'll see File Allocation Table entries displayed in this form: <EOF>, etc.

Press F2 to view the data in HEX format. The blinking cursor is in the upper-left corner. Use the left arrow key to back it up until it is over the upper-leftmost character—go too far and it wraps around to the lower right.

Cure

The first two characters should correspond to the table shown above. They should be followed by FF and, under DOS major Version 3.x, a second FF, provided the partition is larger than 16 megabytes. You don't have to correct the FF's, but note if some other character was present.

Type the media descriptor from the table above as the first two characters, and press PgDn to go to the next sector. Norton asks if you want to write the corrections; answer "W" for write.

There are two copies of the File Allocation Table on the disk. They are supposed to be identical. Usually, when one gets clobbered, so does the other. So we'll have to fix the copy as well.

Press PgDn repeatedly until you see the message "1st sector in 2nd copy of

FAT". It should look just like the first. If it already has an F8 at the start, you can press ESCape until you reach the DOS prompt.

Use the left arrow to back up to the first character in the upper-left corner. Type the media descriptor from the table listed above and press ESCape. Norton asks if you want to write the corrections; answer "W" for write.

Press ESCape until you reach the DOS prompt. Run CHKDSK. All should be well. If not, go back and repeat the steps in this section to see if the changes were made.

Cure

With PC-Tools

Type PCTOOLS drive and press RE-TURN. For example PCTOOLS C: will bring the program up on the C: drive.

Press F3 (selects default Disk Utilities).

Press E for Edit. You'll see half of the first (DOS Boot) sector displayed.

Press PgDn twice. Now you're looking at the first sector of the File Allocation Table.

Press F3 to edit the entries. The blinking cursor is in the upper-left corner.

The first two characters are supposed to correspond to the table above. They should be followed by FF and, under

Cure

DOS major Version 3.x, a second FF, provided the partition is larger than 16 megabytes. You don't have to correct the FF's, but note if some other character was present.

Write down the first six characters, or print the screen with Shift-PrtSc if you have a printer attached. Type in the correct descriptor from the table listing as the first two characters, and press F5 to update and U to confirm.

There are two copies of the File Allocation Table on the disk. They are supposed to be identical. Usually, when one gets clobbered, so does the other. So we'll have to find and fix the copy as well.

The FAT varies in size, otherwise I'd give you a hard figure. The quickest way to find the second copy is to use the F2, chg sector num feature. First use it to select the Root directory area, F2 and "r." Add 1 to the sector number, then divide by 2. Press F2 to change sector number, type the result of your calculation and press RETURN. You should find yourself looking at an identical image of the first sector you corrected.

An alternate approach to finding the second copy of the FAT is this: Press ESCape to get to the main menu. Press F for Find. This lets you enter a search string. But first we need to shift the cursor below the line, to the Hex area. Press F2.

Now, type in the characters you copied before you corrected the first FAT. The more, the better but eight would be plenty. Press RETURN to start searching. You are looking for a match somewhere beyond sector 1 and at offset 0000. If the offset is not zero, press "G" to go on searching.

If this copy of the FAT already has a correct media descriptor at the start, you can press ESCape until you reach the DOS prompt. Otherwise, look up the correct media descriptor in the table above. Correct the first two characters, and press F5 to update and U to confirm.

Press ESCape until you reach the DOS prompt. Run CHKDSK. All should be well. If not, go back and repeat the steps in this section to see if the changes were made.

Cure

"Probable Non-DOS Disk" on a Hard Disk

DIAGNOSIS: File Allocation Table has been altered. The message itself isn't serious, but the implication that something twiddled the FAT deserves attention.

TOOLS REQUIRED: Mace Utilities program NONDOS, or a disk sector editor such as Norton or PC-Tools.

KNOWLEDGE REQUIRED: The first value in the File Allocation Table on any valid DOS media is the Media Descriptor Byte. For fixed disks, this is defined as F8. If something other than F8 is placed there, CHKDSK will complain. If that's all that's wrong, you can continue to run with no problems. Changing the value back to F8 will shut CHKDSK up.

The concern here is that something overwrote a part of the disk that should never be touched except by FDISK or FORMAT. When this happens, you should think about what you've been running on your machine lately, any recent additions to your program library. That new program may not be solely to blame. Quite possibly there is some conflict with resident software or with device drivers declared in your CONFIG.SYS file.

Something, for sure, is not right. Next time the damage might be more extensive. Better to isolate the cause now, but first, back up all your data to floppies or some other drive.

CURE: You could, of course, always reformat the disk with DOS, if you don't mind backing up and restoring all your files.

With Mace

Mace contains a program, NONDOS, that lets you automatically reset the media descriptor to its proper value. Hard disks are virtually always F8.

With Norton 4.0

Type NU drive (or NORTON drive) and press RETURN. For example NU C: will bring the program up on the C: drive.

Press RETURN (selects default Explore Disk).

Press RETURN (selects next default, Choose Item).

Press RETURN (selects default, File).

Press up arrow, then RETURN (selects FAT Area).

Press E for Edit.

You'll see File Allocation Table entries displayed in this form: <EOF>, etc. Press F2 to view the data in HEX format.

The blinking cursor is in the upper-left corner. Use the left arrow key to back it up until it is over the upper-leftmost character—go too far and it wraps around to the lower right.

The first two characters should be F8. They should be followed by FF and, under DOS major Version 3.x, a second FF, provided the partition is larger than 16 megabytes. You don't have to correct the FF's, but note if some other character was present.

Cure

Type "F" and "8" to correct the first two characters, and press PgDn to go to the next sector. Norton asks if you want to write the corrections; answer "W" for write.

There are two copies of the File Allocation Table on the disk. They are supposed to be identical. Usually, when one gets clobbered, so does the other. So we'll have to fix the copy as well.

Press PgDn repeatedly until you see the message "1st sector in 2nd copy of FAT." It should look just like the first. If it already has an F8 at the start, you can press ESCape until you reach the DOS prompt.

Use the left arrow to backup to the first character in the upper-left corner. Type "F" and "8" and press ESCape. Norton asks if you want to write the corrections; answer "W" for write. Press ESCape until you reach the DOS prompt.

Run CHKDSK. All should be well. If not, go back and repeat the steps in this section to see if the changes were made.

Cure

With PC-Tools

Type PCTOOLS drive and press RETURN. For example PCTOOLS C: will bring the program up on the C: drive.

Press F3 (selects default Disk Utilities).

Press E for Edit. You'll see half of the first (DOS Boot) sector displayed.

Press PgDn twice. Now you're looking at the first sector of the File Allocation Table.

Press F3 to edit the entries. The blinking cursor is in the upper-left corner.

The first two characters are supposed to be F8. They should be followed by FF and, under DOS major Version 3.x, a second FF, provided the partition is larger than 16 megabytes. You don't have to correct the FFs, but note if some other character was present.

Write down the first six characters, or print the screen with Shift-PrtSc if you have a printer attached. Type "F" and "8" to correct the first two char-

Cure

acters, and press F5 to update and U to confirm.

There are two copies of the File Allocation Table on the disk. They are supposed to be identical. Usually, when one gets clobbered, so does the other. So we'll have to find and fix the copy as well.

The FAT varies in size, otherwise I'd give you a hard figure. The quickest way to find the second copy is to use the F2, chg sector num feature. First use it to select the Root directory area, F2 and "r." Add 1 to the sector number, then divide by 2. Press F2 to change sector number, type the result of your calculation and press RETURN. You should find yourself looking at an identical image of the first sector you corrected.

An alternate approach to finding the second copy of the FAT is this: Press ESCape get to the main menu. Press "F" for Find. This lets you enter a search string. But first we need to shift the cursor below the line, to the Hex area. Press F2.

Now, type in the characters you copied before you corrected the first FAT. The more, the better, but eight would be plenty. Press RETURN to start searching. You're looking for a match somewhere beyond sector 1 and at offset 0000. If the offset is not zero, press "G" to go on searching.

If this copy of the FAT already has an F8 at the start, you can press ESCape until you reach the DOS prompt. Type "F" and "8" to correct the first two

Cure

characters, and press F5 to update and U to confirm.

Press ESCape until you reach the DOS prompt. Run CHKDSK. All should be well. If not, go back and repeat the steps in this section to see if the changes were made.

"File Not Found" Message. Drive Appears Empty

Mace, Norton Advanced, PC-Tools Deluxe *not* installed.

DIAGNOSIS:

Drive was formatted with DOS. Or FDISK was unintentionally used to re-define partition information. Or you are trying to recover from a low-level disaster.

TOOLS REQUIRED:

Mace Utilities or PC-Tools Deluxe. For drives larger than 32 megabytes, check with the software publisher. Mace 5.0 currently handles up to 512 mega-bytes.

KNOWLEDGE REQUIRED:

Compaq MS-DOS 3.20 or earlier has a lethal FORMAT. So does ATT MS-DOS prior to Version 3.1 release 1.01, and Burroughs MS-DOS. They actually erase the hard disk. You can't recover if FORMAT from one of these versions was used. For the future, you should get a later version of MS-DOS, convert to PC-DOS (which will work just fine), or get Mace, which has separate, non-destructive FORMATs for both hard and floppy disks, and avoid this hap-pening again.

For all other versions of DOS, FOR-MAT.COM doesn't erase the hard disk the way it does floppies; it performs a "logical" format of the disk. This means it reads the entire disk, looking for bad spots, then clears out the old File Allocation Table and marks a fresh one with any bad spots, so they won't be used. Finally, it clears out the root directory. The disk is now *logically* prepared to receive new data, as opposed to a low-level format, which actually marks the disk magnetically into tracks and sectors.

The disk *looks* erased. And, if you go ahead and begin loading fresh data, creating new subdirectories to hold your files, data *is* erased as the new files are recorded over the old information that was still out there. Up to the point that most or all of the original files are recorded over by new files, recovery is possible for all subdirectory information.

Recall, that I said DOS FORMAT clears out the root directory. This is a dedicated area near the start of the DOS partition. All other directories, the ones that branch from the root and from each other, are located somewhere out on the disk. FORMAT doesn't touch them. It is possible for Mace and, more recently, PC-Tools Deluxe, to reattach these subdirectories to the root.

I said the FATs got cleared as well, and that poses a second problem. Without a backup copy of the FAT—the sort provided when Mace, Norton Advanced, or PC-Tools Deluxe is installed—reconstruction of the FAT is a series of educated guesses based on a central hope: that files were not frag-

Knowledge Required

mented. If you regularly run a defragger, such as Mace, Disk Optimizer, Vopt, or others, recovery can be near perfect. Otherwise, some files won't be contiguous, that is, stored in one continuous area physically on the disk, and they will likely not be recovered intact.

The bad news is fragmented files are usually important: frequently modified database, accounting, or word-processing text files. Subdirectories themselves can become fragmented as they grow—again indicating they are probably important—and failure to recover all the pieces can cost you the files they pointed to.

If you are a dBASE user, you might have greater success using dbFix or dSALVAGE, two programs listed in the back of the book, dedicated to fixing and recovering lost or damaged dBASE files. Turn to the section of this book titled dBASE Files Damaged or Lost.

If your most important files are text or word processing files, you might have better luck with TextFix, listed in the back of the book. Norton and PC-Tools also have text retrieval capabilities. All are covered in the section titled Text Files Damaged or Lost.

Knowledge Required

CURE: *With Mace*

Run UnFormat and when it asks you was Mace installed, tell it "no." Recovery is automatic.

Your root directory will contain di-

rectory entries SUB000, SUB001, etc.
You can CD into them, as you would
any DOS directory and a DIR command will show you the files just as
they always appeared.

With PC-Tools Deluxe

Run the program REBUILD. It
searches first for a file created by Mirror, its system backup program, to be
restored. Be patient, it won't find it.
When it asks if you want it to search
the whole disk, type "No." It then
throws you into UnFormat. Tell it
"YES" you want to do this. It will
search the disk, then ask you if you
want to record the results. You must
type "YES" and press Return, or nothing will happen. If you type anything
else, it will abort to the DOS prompt
without recovering data.

Subdirectories in the root will appear as SUBDIR.1, SUBDIR.2, etc. (In
case you hadn't realized it before, yes,
subdirectories can have extensions,
just like any other file.)

All Programs

Run the DOS program CHKDSK, no
matter which program you used. Normally no errors will be reported. If
there are errors, note which files are
referred to. They were probably not recovered intact.

Run CHKDSK with the /F option un-

Cure

Cure

til no errors are reported. If you see a ". . . convert to files, yes or no." message, answer "y" for yes. These files will show up in the root with the .CHK extension. They may represent intact files. Read the section of this book titled Using DOS CHKDSK. Use the Mace RENDIR command to rename the directories to their original name.

You should methodically examine all your programs and associated data files before you continue using the disk. If they're not intact, now is the time to find the missing pieces, before you copy or delete anything. Read the sections titled Disk Sector Editors, and Data Files Damaged or Lost.

With Mace you may have some extra directories—these were fragments UnFormat located. You'll have to copy the files back to their original directories and delete and remove the recovered fragment. You may also have some new files in the root that were once in subdirectories. Copy these back to where they belong, then delete the root directory entries.

If program files are damaged— the application hangs or behaves strangely—install a fresh copy from the original disk. Copy protected software such as Lotus 1-2-3 will no doubt require reinstallation. Unless you have a company policy against it, now would be a good time to buy Copy-Write or UnLock, and deprotect your software. Or ask Lotus for an unprotected version.

Now, make a complete backup of all

your data. At least copy your valuable files to some other drive or to floppy disk and put them away.

If the DOS program FDISK was used, you may be missing one or more files of pieces of subdirectory. Under DOS major Version 3.x, FDISK not only initializes the disk partition information, it does a read/write test of the data area where it wants to put the system files and Command.com. It takes a rather generous swipe, erasing whatever was there.

Cure

If you're the sort of person who creates the most important subdirectory first, you may have lost all or part of it to FDISK. Your only recourse at this point is to read the sections Disk Sector Editors, and Data Files Damaged or Lost.

In Case of Failure

A DOS 2.x drive formatted with DOS 3.x won't recover successfully. You'll have to dig out your DOS 2.x disk and re-FDISK and re-FORMAT, then start over again with this section.

Be advised, DOS has grown. More importantly, DOS 3.x has much larger FATs than DOS 2.x. This means some data, possibly important files or directories have no doubt been erased. There is nothing to be done about that now except cross your fingers and hope.

A DOS 3.x drive formatted with a later version of DOS may, again, be missing valuable data or directories.

Cure

DOS keeps growing. If the /S option was specified, you may have clobbered as much as 20K of data.

SUMMARY:

With the exception of certain earlier versions of Compaq, ATT, and Burroughs DOS, FORMAT is a recoverable situation. Fragmentation of files or the use of FDISK, or FORMAT with later versions of DOS than that originally used can significantly cripple recovery. But experience shows seven out of ten files will, on average, be recovered intact. You may do better or worse. But any data recovered is data you don't have to recreate.

You should seriously consider installing Mace, or Norton Advanced, or PC-Tools Deluxe, to allow quick recovery in the future. If you choose Mace or PC-Tools Deluxe, you can remove FORMAT from the disk, as each comes with a dedicated floppy format program. After all, you don't ordinarily need a hard disk format program on your hard disk.

"File Not Found" Message.
Drive Appears Empty

Mace, Norton Advanced, or PC-Tools Deluxe *was* installed.

DIAGNOSIS: Drive was formatted with DOS. Or FDISK was used unintentionally to re-define partition information. Or you're trying to recover from some low-level disaster.

TOOLS REQUIRED: Mace Utilities, Norton Advanced, or PC-Tools Deluxe. For drives larger than 32 megabytes, check with the software publisher. Mace 5.0 currently handles up to 512 megabytes.

KNOWLEDGE REQUIRED: Compaq MS-DOS 3.20 or earlier has a lethal FORMAT. So does ATT MS-DOS prior to Version 3.1 Release 1.01, and Burroughs MS-DOS. They actually erase the hard disk. You can't recover if FORMAT from one of these versions was used, even if protective software was installed. For the future, you should get a later version of MS-DOS, convert to PC-DOS (which will work just fine), or get Mace, which has sep-arate, nondestructive FORMATs for both hard and floppy disks, and avoid this happening again.

For all other versions of DOS, FOR-MAT.COM doesn't erase the hard disk

Knowledge Required

the way it does floppies; it performs a *logical* format of the disk. This means it reads the entire disk, looking for bad spots, then clears out the old File Allocation Table, and marks a fresh one with any bad spots, so they won't be used. Finally, it clears out the root directory. The disk is now logically prepared to receive new data, as opposed to a low-level format, which actually marks the disk magnetically into tracks and sectors.

The disk *looks* erased. And, if you go ahead and begin loading fresh data, creating new subdirectories to hold your files, data is erased as the new files are recorded over the old information that was still out there. Up to the point that most or all of the original files are recorded over by new files, recovery is possible for all subdirectory information.

Recall that I said DOS FORMAT clears out the root directory. This is a dedicated area near the start of the DOS partition. All other directories, the ones that branch from the root and from each other, are located somewhere out on the disk. FORMAT doesn't touch them. It is possible for Mace, PC-Tools Deluxe, and Norton Advanced to recover, because each provides a program that, usually at power-up, makes a copy of the DOS boot, FAT, and root directory. That copy lies elsewhere on the disk, where FORMAT won't touch it. Restoring it will bring the drive back to where it was when the copy was made, or close to it.

The exception to perfect recovery involves work done after the backup program ran. If a file was created, copied, grew, or DOS moved it (quite common under DOS major Version 3.x) it won't be perfectly recovered. Something may be missing from the end, or you may get back an earlier revision.

The bad news is, the moved files are usually important: frequently modified database, accounting or word-processing text files.

If you're a dBASE user, you might have greater success using dbFix or dSALVAGE, two programs listed in the back of the book, dedicated to fixing and recovering lost or damaged dBASE files. Turn to the section of this book titled dBASE Files Damaged or Lost.

If your most important files are text or word processing files, you might have better luck with TextFix, listed in the back of the book. Norton and PC-Tools also have text retrieval capabilities. All are covered in the section titled Text Files Damaged or Lost.

Knowledge Required

CURE: *With Mace*

Run UnFormat and when it asks you was Mace installed, tell it "yes." It'll search the disk for all current and older copies of the backup file. All are date-time stamped and will be identified as either "current" or "old." Don't worry about how UnFormat can find the file without a directory. It knows what it's looking for, and it knows where it was stored, even if it was fragmented.

When it finds a copy, it stops, shows you the information and asks if you want it restored. Normally, you want the current file, BACKUP.M_U, and would say "no" to other choices. Restoration is automatic.

Cure

With PC-Tools Deluxe

Run REBUILD. It searches a dedicated area of the disk for a file created by MIRROR, usually at power-on or reboot. If it can't locate it, it asks permission to search the entire disk.

With Norton Advanced

Run FR, Format Recovery. It searches for and restores a file created with the FR /SAVE option, usually at boot time.

All Programs

No matter which program you used, run the DOS program CHKDSK. Normally no, or few, errors will be reported. If there are errors, note which files are referred to. They were probably modified after the backup file was last updated.

Run CHKDSK with the /F option until no errors are reported. If you see a "... convert to files, yes or no." message, answer "y" for yes. These files will show up in the root with the .CHK extension. They may represent intact files. Read the section of this book titled Using DOS CHKDSK. Use the Mace RENDIR command to rename the directories to their original name.

You should methodically examine all your programs and associated data files before you continue to use the disk. If they're not intact, now is the time to find the missing pieces, before you copy or delete anything. Read the section titled Data Files Damaged or Lost.

Cure

If program files are damaged—the application hangs or behaves strangely—install a fresh copy from the original disk. Copy protected software such as Lotus 1-2-3 will no doubt require reinstallation. Unless you have a company policy against it, now would be a good time to buy Copy-Write or UnLock, and deprotect your software.

Now, make a complete backup of all your data. At least copy your valuable files to some other drive or to floppy disk and put them away.

You should seriously consider making up batch files to enter and exit important applications, with the last line of the batch procedure a call to RXBAK, MIRROR, or FR, depending on whether you own Mace, Norton Advanced, or PC-Tools Deluxe. This insures recovery information will be current for all important data, and only adds a few seconds to the time it takes you to get in and out of a program.

If you have Mace or PC-Tools Deluxe, you can remove DOS FORMAT

Cure

from the disk, as each comes with a dedicated floppy format program. After all, you don't ordinarily need a hard disk format program on your hard disk.

SUMMARY:

Once Mace's RXBAK, PC-Tools Deluxe's MIRROR or Norton Advanced's FR /SAVE is installed, FORMAT recovery, and recovery from other low-level disasters, is greatly improved—possibly even perfect. The key to perfection is how frequently you execute the backup program to update the boot, FAT, and root directory information.

Recovery from FORMAT, FDISK or other low-level disasters can be hampered by crossing versions of DOS, especially using DOS 3.x on a disk previously setup under DOS 2.x. FDISK also does some extra nasty things that may reduce your success rate.

"File Not Found" Message. Directory Entry Appears to Be DELeted or ERASEd

Recovery with Mace Utilities.

DIAGNOSIS:

Usually DOS wildcard characters were used to delete or erase something, and valuable files disappeared as a consequence, unintentionally.

TOOLS REQUIRED:

Mace Utilities UnDelete.

KNOWLEDGE REQUIRED:

The only way you can destroy data after deleting it is to put new data on the disk or diskette. If you just deleted *.* and pressed ENTER, everything is still there. True, the longer you continued working after you erased something, the less likely you are to get all your information back, but there is always the possibility that some, if not all, your data is intact, even if hours, days, or weeks have passed before you caught the goof. So stop, immediately!

The DELete and ERASE commands are identical in operation and effect. Both cause an entry to disappear from the disk directory, and an equivalent amount of free storage space to be added to the number you see at the end of a DIR command. That's all the DEL and ERASE commands do. They don't actually wipe files off the disk.

Deleting something is the equivalent of tearing the label off an audio or video cassette. You (and DOS) no longer know what's on it, or where it's located, but it's still there until you record over it. UnDeleting is simply the reconstruction of a new directory label and remapping the location of the data to the FAT. The first part's easy, and several people do it besides Mace. The remapping part, however, can get tricky. There are some situations, when the file wasn't stored physically in one place on the disk, where programs such as Norton's QU—Quick UnErase—don't correctly recover the data. Mace does, and so, more recently, does PC-Tools Deluxe, which is covered in the next section.

The second thing DOS does when you delete a file is erase the map of where it was stored, effectively saying "this space is free" for later use. As I said before, the good news is *the map is not the data!* It's a separate table, called the File Allocation Table (FAT), that points to the data. If you want to know more about FATs, read Chapter 1. For now, it's enough to know that for every physical area of the disk where data is stored, there's a corresponding entry in the FAT. Before writing to the disk, DOS looks to the FAT to determine what free space is available. When you erase something, DOS clears the corresponding mapped area in the

Knowledge Required

Knowledge Required

FAT. Afterwards, it interprets the now empty area in the FAT to mean the corresponding area of the disk may be safely be re-recorded.

While this indirection may seem tedious or confusing to you—the directory points to the FAT, the FAT points to the data—computer programmers regard this kind of construction as elegant: simple, effective, straightforward. Compared to the past (CP/M) and the future (OS/2 extended file systems), or current alternatives, such as Unix, the DOS file structure, with simple Directories and one FAT, is a breeze to comprehend. Credit the elegance to Marc MacDonald and Bill Gates, in the early days at Microsoft, where they invented the scheme for disk BASIC.

If the erased file was stored in a single place on the disk, that is, it occupied consecutive entries in the FAT, quick recovery is potentially easy, and all UnDeleters work alike. They take the old start address in the Directory, then look in the FAT. If the FAT says that area is available for recording data, the program counts the number of consecutive empty FAT entries and compares them to the original file size in the deleted directory entry. If available space equals file size, the UnDelete or UnErase program reasons this must be the place where your file was, and it simply rewrites the FAT to show that space once more occupied, with the last FAT entry marked to indicate the End-of-File.

Knowledge Required

You're prompted for a replacement character for the file name, and the corrected directory (no more) now points to a filled-in FAT and the FAT points to the data on the physical disk. If nothing has been re-recorded, what's there is the original data, and, from DOS's point of view, the file is now just as it was before you deleted it. The DIR command lists the file, and you may use it in your programs and manipulate it with DOS commands.

Seven out of ten times, that's the way it works, and it works well with all UnErase and Undelete programs. The problem is, DOS doesn't guarantee that it'll store any given file in one physical piece on the disk. Each space in the FAT represents only one storage segment of the disk, and a file may occupy any number of segments in any order. It may, in fact, be scattered all over the place, that is, randomly, segmented, or fragmented.

One beauty of the FAT is that it allows DOS to add, delete, alter, and retrieve files without wasting disk space. The highest priority, established long ago when on-line mass storage devices were relatively expensive, is assigned to minimizing wasted storage. In a conflict of storage interests, keeping files contiguous always takes second-place with DOS.

Never assume a deleted file was in one piece. Therefore, never assume that an UnDeleted or UnErased file is intact until you've looked at it closely from beginning to end. The exceptions are

Knowledge Required

Mace UnDelete and, more recently, PC-Tools Deluxe.

The most important piece of information lost when you delete a file is its location in the FAT map. Many experts waste hours, even days trying to manually reconstruct the FAT for valuable files that were stored randomly on the disk. This is rarely necessary when Mace Utilities were previously installed and RXBAK running. RXBAK, among other things, makes a spare copy of the FAT against disaster. Mace UnDelete references this older, duplicate copy of the FAT. In most instances where you've just deleted something and haven't rebooted the machine, or turned it off and on again, Mace can compare the directory start location to the original map entries, and rewrite the FAT accurately, no matter how fragmented the file was. Under DOS major Version 2.x, contiguity is never considered, and files tend to be highly segmented.

Under DOS 3.x, a stab was made at keeping things in one piece, with interesting implications for recovery. Large files, and especially files that are constantly undergoing change, such as database files, still tend to fragment rapidly and recurrently. But DOS 3.x tends to move things around on the disk without telling you, so there may be previous versions of a file in unallocated areas of the disk. That's worth knowing when all else fails and the only hope is to rebuild a file from scratch with raw data from the disk.

Seven in ten isn't a bad average in baseball, but when it comes to recovering deleted data it's bush league. Any failure rate is too high when the one file you wanted back is the one you didn't get. This stuff is valuable if only in terms of the time spent entering it into the computer. So, lets talk about the less than ideal situations.

When an UnDelete or UnErase program compares the old start address in the directory with the corresponding map entry in the FAT, it hopes to find a single, unallocated sequence that represents original file size or greater, in available storage. If that fails to be the case, the program usually presumes the file was fragmented. Some initial portion of the file is located but the rest was stored elsewhere, and lacking any idea what the old FAT map looked like, quick recovery is out of the question.

Mace, and the latest editions of Norton and PC-Tools Deluxe, allow you to piece together a file manually. The procedure for recovering a fragmented files is one of searching, reviewing, and saving. Most importantly, you should always try to *recover data to some other drive*. Never recover files to the same drive from which you're trying to retrieve them. The smaller the file, the higher the success rate.

Knowledge Required

CURE: As always, my first advice is to STOP! Take your hands off the keyboard, get a grip on the edge, and push yourself away from your desk.

You may want to get any oaths, curses, or expletives out of your system right away. Prayer at this juncture is also often soothing, though it's not clear whether God understands computers better than mortals. Just don't hit any keys. (Don't hit *anything*; you may want two good hands before you're finished.)

The first thing all UnDelete and UnErase programs do is look for vestiges of the old label—the directory entry. When you erase a file, DOS marks the lead character in the directory entry with a little sigma. Thereafter, it won't display it when you type DIR.

The rest of the entry is left intact, and this provides us with some valuable information: the date and time the file was created, its length, and where it originally started on the map of the physical disk.

Cure

The first step in recovery is to correct that to some other character. Most people prefer the original letter. DOS doesn't care, so long as it's not one of the prohibited characters (.?/*\ or space). It just has to be something other than sigma, σ.

Mace UnDelete shows you a listing of all deleted references. As you highlight the entries with the arrow keys, you see their status, that is, an indication of how likely you are to recover.

Quick UnDelete

If Mace is installed and RXBAK runs at power-up or reboot time, there is a

Cure

copy of the old File Allocation Table in BACKUP.M_U. There is an extremely high probability that UnDelete has located the correct FAT information that DOS threw away. Even though the file may have been fragmented, an accurate FAT can be reconstructed and quick recovery is highly likely to be perfect. Still, you should check the file for accuracy before continuing.

If Mace wasn't installed, the program determines there's enough vacant space where the file used to be to have held it. In other words, everything looks like it fits and no one currently owns the area where the data were stored. So quick recovery is possible. The shorter the file, the higher the probability it'll be recovered intact.

There is no penalty for Quick Un-Delete. If you check the file and find it wasn't recovered intact, you can always delete it again and take the more cautious approach.

When UnDelete asks "Quick Un-Delete—(Yes/No)" press "y" for yes. UnDelete then asks for a new first character for the filename. Any valid filename character will suffice. Recovery proceeds automatically. The file will be listed as it always was.

Check it for integrity. It is possible that BACKUP.M_U was updated *after* you deleted the file. Fear not, for unless you disabled it, RXBAK keeps the previous copy around as OLDBACK.M_U. You can copy OLDBACK.M_U to BACKUP.M_U and try again.

Probably Fragmented

This status shows that some other file now occupies part of the disk where the deleted file once began. This could mean data have been erased, but more often it means the original file wasn't stored in one physical piece. It was fragmented around the disk. Either the information in BACKUP.M_U is invalid, or Mace wasn't installed. You'll have to recover manually, using the search and save features of UnDelete.

Recovering text or word processing files is relatively easy. Database files are harder—dBASE users can look up the special section on recovering dBASE files. Recovering large spreadsheets can be nerve wracking—Lotus users should look up 1-2-3 recovery. Recovering program files is pointless—get fresh copies off the original disks. Recovering copy protected files is impossible. You should get Copy-Write or UnLock to deprotect the originals, and reinstall. Lotus is now handing out a free utility for unlocking 1-2-3.

UnDelete will strongly urge you to put the file somewhere else—that is, recover to another drive. It is not good practice to be altering a drive with lost data on it, when you have no idea how successful you might be. You may have to try several times before getting it right. Large files may prove difficult, but you can save them in floppy-sized chunks and then put them back together with the concatenate feature of

Cure

Cure

the DOS COPY command, which I'll explain a little bit further on.

Undelete shows you the data area of the disk where the erased file used to start—note PLACE at the top of the screen is set to 1. You may return here after exploring. You can save what you're looking at (and all the other sectors of data associated with it on the disk) by pressing RETURN. You can then use the arrow keys, or F1 TEXT SEARCH, to locate the next piece of data belonging to this file. Press RETURN and it will be tacked onto the end of the first piece.

F1 text search looks at the entire disk beyond where you are, then ahead of where you are. While you expect the next piece of data to come *after* the one you're looking at, that isn't always the case. DOS can put things anywhere it finds free space, so don't be surprised when a search finds the data stored *before* the current place, possibly even ahead of PLACE = 1.

Normally, UnDelete shows you only "deleted" areas of the disk, so you won't have to wade through data that belongs to active files.

Probably Erased

When an active file occupies the space once allocated to an erased file, UnDelete declares the deleted file truly erased. A fragment—possibly all but the first data cluster—may still exist. If so, you can follow the previous drill for searching and capturing fragmented data. Or you might want to search for a previous copy of the file; while outdated, it may be valuable.

Cure

File Not Listed

If you did some work after erasing the file, it's possible that DOS reused the directory slot but didn't actually write over the file's data on the disk. This is likely under DOS major Version 3.x. Choose any filename in Undelete, then ignore where it wants to start. Simply search for the start of the file that interests you and begin there. You can rename the file after you've captured it. For the most part, files do not "know" their own names and DOS couldn't care less, so long as the name doesn't contain prohibited characters (.?*|\/<>). Recovery procedure is the same as it was for fragmented files.

Undeleting Directories

Directories, as I've said elsewhere, are simply files that contain directory information. With the exception of the root directory, they all begin with two special entries, . and .., and are easy to recognize.

Two things make Undeleting a directory different. The first piece must have . and .. entries. And all the other entries will show as deleted, the first character replaced with a sigma.

Cure

That's because, of course, DOS forces you to delete everything before letting you remove the directory. If you use a search to find the directory entries, don't search for the whole filename; omit the first letter, or use a "?," which will match anything, including the sigma. Once recovered, the directory will still look empty from DOS's perspective. You'll have to Undelete the files one at a time.

Second, because DOS doesn't keep track of the size of a directory. There's no automatic way of knowing when it's fully recovered, except that the last piece usually (but not always) has some unused slots. It's up to you to determine that all the files in the directory are accounted for.

"File Not Found" Message. Directory Entry Appears to Be DELeted or ERASEd

Recovery with Norton Utilities.

DIAGNOSIS:

Usually DOS wildcard characters were used to delete or erase something, and valuable files disappeared as a consequence, unintentionally.

TOOLS REQUIRED:

Norton Utilities Quick UnErase (QU) or NU.

KNOWLEDGE REQUIRED:

The only way you can destroy data after deleting it is to put new data on the disk or diskette. If you just deleted *.* and pressed ENTER, everything is still there. True, the longer you continued working after you erased something, the less likely you are to get all your information back, but there is always the possibility that some, if not all, of your data is intact, even if hours, days, or weeks have passed before you caught the goof. So stop, immediately!

The DELete and ERASE commands are identical in operation and effect. Both cause an entry to disappear from the disk directory, and an equivalent amount of free storage space to be added to the number you see at the end

Knowledge Required

of a DIR command. That's all the DEL and ERASE commands do. They don't actually wipe files off the disk.

Deleting something is the equivalent of tearing the label off an audio or video cassette. You (and DOS) no longer know what's on it, or where it's located, but it's still there until you record over it. UnDeleting is simply the reconstruction of a new directory label and remapping the location of the data to the FAT. The first part's easy, and several people do it besides Mace. The remapping part, however, can get tricky. There are some situations, when the file wasn't stored physically in one place on the disk, where programs such as Norton's QU—Quick UnErase—don't correctly recover the data. Mace does, and so, more recently, does PC-Tools Deluxe, which is covered in the next section.

The second thing DOS does when you delete a file is erase the map of where it was stored, effectively saying "this space is free" for later use. As I said before, the good news is *the map is not the data!* It's a separate table, called the File Allocation Table (FAT), that points to the data. If you want to know more about FATs, read Chapter 1. For now, it's enough to know that for every physical area of the disk where data is stored, there's a corresponding entry in the FAT. Before writing to the disk, DOS looks to the FAT to determine what free space is available. When you erase something, DOS clears the corresponding mapped area in the

FAT. Afterwards, it interprets the now empty area in the FAT to mean the corresponding area of the disk may be safely be re-recorded.

While this indirection may seem tedious or confusing to you—the directory points to the FAT, the FAT points to the data—computer programmers regard this kind of construction as elegant: simple, effective, straightforward. Compared to the past (CP/M) and the future (OS/2 extended file systems), or current alternatives, such as Unix, the DOS file structure, with simple Directories and one FAT, is a breeze to comprehend. Credit the elegance to Marc MacDonald and Bill Gates, in the early days at Microsoft, where they invented the scheme for disk BASIC.

Knowledge Required

If the erased file was stored in a single place on the disk, that is, it occupied consecutive entries in the FAT, quick recovery is potentially easy, and all UnDeleters work alike. They take the old start address in the Directory, then look in the FAT. If the FAT says that area is available for recording data, the program counts the number of consecutive empty FAT entries and compares them to the original file size in the deleted directory entry. If available space equals file size, the UnDelete or UnErase program reasons this must be the place where your file was, and it simply rewrites the FAT to show that space once more occupied, with the last FAT entry marked to indicate the End-of-File.

You're prompted for a replacement

character for the file name, and the corrected directory (no more) now points to a filled-in FAT and the FAT points to the data on the physical disk. If nothing has been re-recorded, what's there is the original data, and, from DOS's point of view, the file is now just as it was before your deleted it. The DIR command lists the file, and you may use it in your programs and manipulate it with DOS commands.

Seven out of ten times, that's the way it works, and it works well with all UnErase and Undelete programs. The problem is, DOS doesn't guarantee that it'll store any given file in one physical piece on the disk. Each space in the FAT represents only one storage segment of the disk, and a file may occupy any number of segments in any order. It may, in fact, be scattered all over the place, that is, randomly, segmented, or fragmented.

One beauty of the FAT is that it allows DOS to add, delete, alter, and retrieve files without wasting disk space. The highest priority, established long ago when on-line mass storage devices were relatively expensive, is assigned to minimizing wasted storage. In a conflict of storage interests, keeping files contiguous always takes second-place with DOS.

Never assume a deleted file was in one piece. Therefore, never assume that an UnDeleted or UnErased file is intact until you've looked at it closely from beginning to end. The exceptions are Mace UnDelete and, more recently,

Knowledge Required

Knowledge Required

PC-Tools Deluxe. Norton will no doubt soon follow suit.

The most important piece of information lost when you delete a file is its location in the FAT map. Many experts waste hours, even days trying to manually reconstruct the FAT for valuable files that were stored randomly on the disk. This is rarely necessary when Mace Utilities were previously installed and RXBAK running. RXBAK, among other things, makes a spare copy of the FAT against disaster. Mace UnDelete references this older, duplicate copy of the FAT. In most instances where you've just deleted something, and haven't rebooted the machine, or turned it off and on again, Mace can compare the directory start location to the original map entries, and rewrite the FAT accurately, no matter how fragmented the file was. Under DOS major Version 2.x, contiguity is never considered, and files tend to be highly segmented.

Under DOS 3.x, a stab was made at keeping things in one piece, with interesting implications for recovery. Large files, and especially files that are constantly undergoing change, such as database files, still tend to fragment rapidly and recurrently. But DOS 3.x tends to move things around on the disk without telling you, so there may be previous versions of a file in unallocated areas of the disk. That's worth knowing when all else fails and the only hope is to rebuild a file from scratch with raw data from the disk.

Seven in ten isn't a bad average in baseball, but when it comes to recovering deleted data it's bush league. Any failure rate is too high when the one file you wanted back is the one you didn't get. This stuff is valuable if only in terms of the time spent entering it into the computer. So, lets talk about the less than ideal situations.

When an UnDelete or UnErase program compares the old start address in the directory with the corresponding map entry in the FAT, it hopes to find a single, unallocated sequence that represents original file size or greater, in available storage. If that fails to be the case, the program usually presumes the file was fragmented. Some initial portion of the file is located but the rest was stored elsewhere, and lacking any idea what the old FAT map looked like, quick recovery is out of the question.

Mace, and the latest editions of Norton and PC-Tools Deluxe, allow you to piece together a file manually. The procedure for recovering a fragmented file is one of searching, reviewing and saving. Most importantly, you should always try to *recover data to some other drive*. Never recover files to the same drive from which you're trying to retrieve them. The smaller the file, the higher the success rate.

Knowledge Required

CURE: As always, my first advice is to STOP! Take your hands off the keyboard, get a grip on the edge, and push yourself away from your desk.

You may want to get any oaths, curses, or expletives out of your system right away. Prayer at this juncture is also often soothing, though it's not clear whether God understands computers better than mortals. Just don't hit any keys. (Don't hit *anything*; you may want two good hands before you're finished.)

Cure

Quick Unerase

Norton has a separate utility for "quick" Unerasing and undeleting, called QU or Quick Unerase. You can supply it a pathname, or run it in the directory where your lost file was located. It will lead you one at a time through deleted files it thinks can be safely recovered. As of this writing, Norton doesn't make use of the backup information used for Format recovery, making QU a potentially dangerous tool. Fragmented files won't be recovered intact and you won't know about it unless you check each file thoroughly. If you want to use QU, be sure to check your files and immediately delete any that aren't completely intact.

Unerase

This is part of the main utility, NORTON (or NU).

From the main menu, press **U** for Unerase. Press **S** for select file.

Use the arrow keys to high-light

Cure

your file in the list. The first character is missing, because DOS replaced it with a sigma to denote erasure. You must replace it with some legitimate character. Normally it doesn't matter what that character is, unless you are working with accounting software or some other package that is religiously linked to a certain named file. DOS doesn't care. You can even select the first option, "create file" and make up a filename to recover data to.

When filling in the missing letter, the starting cluster is listed near the top. Write it down. If you go exploring you may need to come back to this spot on the disk.

The main recovery menu gives you a number of ways of tracking down your data. Since there's no real penalty, you will probably want to "Add new clusters" and take "All clusters automatically" to see how lucky you are. You can then "Examine/Edit selected clusters" and see if you got what you wanted.

If recovered pieces are simply out of sequence, you can highlight the errant cluster listed at the bottom of the screen and press RETURN, then move to the cluster number it goes ahead of and press RETURN again to insert it there.

Norton Unerase works by making up a new FAT chain as you select and order data. It's not modifying your disk—not until you say so. It is keeping track of which cluster goes where. When you tell it to "Save erased file" it creates a new set of FAT entries and fixes the missing character in the directory.

Typically, if you don't get what you want with the automatic recovery, you'll have to search for data. Find the first piece of your file by searching for some key word. Add that cluster. Now, look at the end of what you've saved. If it breaks in the middle of a word and you know what that word was, search for the missing piece.

Say the found fragment ends with "ho" and you know from context that this is the word "hotel." Search for the fragment "tel." You expect to find it at the start of another cluster. No other match counts. When you find "tel," add that cluster, go to the end again and repeat the search for the missing fragment. If there is no break in the last word, you'll have to guess at what must have come next.

Cure

I encourage you to be procedural about this. It takes less time in the long run. Think of this as an archaeological dig. You could just shovel up a bunch of pieces and use the "move cluster" option to rearrange them, but this can lead to other unnecessary nightmares. Better to pick up one piece at a time.

I presume you're recovering text or something with text in it, like a database or worksheet file. Since it's likely there have been a number of revisions, it's equally probable that the deleted areas of the disk contain more than one whole or fragmentary copy of the data. The differences may be subtle, so go slow. If you change your mind, or stumble on a more recent copy of the data, capture it, move it to the right position, then delete the older cluster. Remember, *you aren't altering the disk*, you're telling Norton what data on the disk to link up in the FAT and in what order.

When the "Clusters found" and "Clusters needed" numbers on the recovery menu agree, and review indicates all the data you want are recovered in proper sequence, you can "Save erased file," escape to DOS, and try loading the file into an application to work on it.

Cure

If the file won't load, you'll have to delete it and start over. You may be missing something from the head or tail of the file. Spreadsheet and database files in particular usually have "header" information preceding the first recognizable data. This often includes things you might recognize, such as the filename, a creation date, field definitions, and printer defaults. Similarly, there may be data following the last recognizable text, so make sure you don't throw away a few lines of information at the end, thinking you'll retype them; along with them, you may have left out important tables your program needs to interpret the data. If "needed" and "found" didn't agree, this is certainly the case; if they did agree, you may have picked up and mixed in obsolete copies of the data alongside current copies. Try again and pay close attention to the splices, that is, the places where one cluster adjoins another.

Cure

File Not Listed

If you did some work after erasing the file, it's possible that DOS reused the directory slot but didn't actually write over the file's data on the disk. This is likely under DOS major Version 3.x. Choose "create file" at the top of the file list. Make up a name, then simply search for the start of the file that interests you and begin there. You can rename the file after you've captured it. For the most part, files don't "know" their own names, and DOS couldn't care less, so long as the name doesn't contain prohibited characters (.?*|\ <>). Recovery is the same as it was for fragmented files, a manual procedure.

Unerasing Directories

Directories, as I've said elsewhere, are simply files that contain directory information. With the exception of the root directory, they all begin with two special entries, . and .. and are easy to recognize. Norton provides a special utility, UR (UnRemove) for restoring erased directories.

Two things make Unerasing a directory different. The first piece must have . and .. entries. And all the other entries will show as deleted, the first character replaced with a sigma. That's because, of course, DOS forces you to delete everything before letting you remove the directory. If you use a search to find the directory entries, don't search for the whole filename; omit the first letter, or use a "?," which will match anything, including the sigma. Once recovered, the directory will still look empty from DOS's perspective. You'll have to Unerase the files one at a time.

Second, because DOS doesn't keep track of the size of a directory, there's no automatic way of knowing when it's fully recovered, except that the last piece usually (but not always) has some unused slots. It's up to you to determine that all the files in the directory are accounted for.

Cure

SUMMARY:

Norton's Quick Unerase will often fail on fragmented files, so be sure to check the recovered files for accuracy before continuing. Presumably, in some later release, Norton will begin to use his backup information as I do, and this will be more reliable.

Normal Unerase involves identifying and piecing together clusters of data. It relies on your ability to make enough sense of the data to ensure an accurate sequence. Unerase takes care of actually reconstructing the File Al-

Cure

location Table and directory entry based on the way you say things should look. This can be a trial and error process, but any data you can locate can be turned into a valid file.

"File Not Found" Message. Directory Entry Appears to Be DELeted or ERASEd

Recovery with PC-Tools.

DIAGNOSIS: Usually DOS wildcard characters were used to delete or erase something, and valuable files disappeared as a consequence, unintentionally.

TOOLS REQUIRED: PC-Tools Deluxe.

KNOWLEDGE REQUIRED: The only way you can destroy data after deleting it is to put new data on the disk or diskette. If you just deleted *.* and pressed ENTER, everything is still there. True, the longer you continued working after you erased something, the less likely you are to get all your information back, but there is always the possibility that some, if not all, of your data is intact, even if hours, days or weeks have passed before you caught the goof. So stop immediately!

The DELete and ERASE commands are identical in operation and effect. Both cause an entry to disappear from the disk directory, and an equivalent amount of free storage space to be added to the number you see at the end of a DIR command. That's all the DEL and ERASE commands do. They don't actually wipe files off the disk.

Deleting something is the equivalent of tearing the label off an audio or video cassette. You (and DOS) no longer know what's on it, or where it's located, but it's still there until you record over it. UnDeleting is simply the reconstruction of a new directory label and remapping the location of the data to the FAT. The first part's easy, and several people do it besides Mace. The remapping part, however, can get tricky. There are some situations, when the file wasn't stored physically in one place on the disk, where programs such as Norton's QU—Quick UnErase—don't correctly recover the data. Mace does, and so, more recently, does PC-Tools Deluxe, which is covered in the next section.

The second thing DOS does when you delete a file is erase the map of where it was stored, effectively saying "this space is free" for later use. As I said before, the good news is *the map is not the data!* It's a separate table, called the File Allocation Table (FAT), that points to the data. If you want to know more about FATs, read Chapter 1. For now, it's enough to know that for every physical area of the disk where data is stored, there's a corresponding entry in the FAT. Before writing to the disk, DOS looks to the FAT to determine what free space is available. When you erase something, DOS clears the corresponding mapped area in the FAT. Afterwards, it interprets the now

Knowledge Required

Knowledge Required

empty area in the FAT to mean the corresponding area of the disk may be safely be re-recorded.

While this indirection may seem tedious or confusing to you—the directory points to the FAT, the FAT points to the data—computer programmers regard this kind of construction as elegant: simple, effective, straightforward. Compared to the past (CP/M) and the future (OS/2 extended file systems), or current alternatives, such as Unix, the DOS file structure, with simple Directories and one FAT, is a breeze to comprehend. Credit the elegance to Marc MacDonald and Bill Gates, in the early days at Microsoft, where they invented the scheme for disk BASIC.

If the erased file was stored in a single place on the disk, that is, it occupied consecutive entries in the FAT, quick recovery is potentially easy, and all UnDeleters work alike. They take the old start address in the Directory, then look in the FAT. If the FAT says that area is available for recording data, the program counts the number of consecutive empty FAT entries and compares them to the original file size in the deleted directory entry. If available space equals file size, the UnDelete or UnErase program reasons this must be the place where your file was, and it simply rewrites the FAT to show that space once more occupied, with the last FAT entry marked to indicate the End-of-File.

You're prompted for a replacement character for the file name, and the corrected directory (no more) now points to a filled-in FAT and the FAT points to the data on the physical disk. If nothing has been re-recorded, what's there is the original data, and, from DOS's point of view, the file is now just as it was before you deleted it. The DIR command lists the file, and you may use it in your programs and manipulate it with DOS commands.

Seven out of ten times, that's the way it works, and it works well with all UnErase and UnDelete programs. The problem is, DOS doesn't guarantee that it'll store any given file in one physical piece on the disk. Each space in the FAT represents only one storage segment of the disk, and a file may occupy any number of segments in any order. It may, in fact, be scattered all over the place, that is, randomly, segmented or fragmented.

One beauty of the FAT is that it allows DOS to add, delete, alter, and retrieve files without wasting disk space. The highest priority, established long ago when on-line mass storage devices were relatively expensive, is assigned to minimizing wasted storage. In a conflict of storage interests, keeping files contiguous always takes second-place with DOS.

Never assume a deleted file was in one piece. Therefore, never assume that an UnDeleted or UnErased file is intact until you've looked at it closely from beginning to end. The exceptions are Mace UnDelete and, more recently, PC-Tools Deluxe.

Knowledge Required

Knowledge Required

The most important piece of information lost when you delete a file is its location in the FAT map. Many experts waste hours, even days trying to manually reconstruct the FAT for valuable files that were stored randomly on the disk. This is rarely necessary when Mace Utilities were previously installed and RXBAK running. RXBAK, among other things, makes a spare copy of the FAT against disaster. Mace UnDelete references this older, duplicate copy of the FAT. In most instances where you've just deleted something, and haven't rebooted the machine, or turned it off and on again, Mace can compare the directory start location to the original map entries, and rewrite the FAT accurately, no matter how fragmented the file was. Under DOS major Version 2.x, contiguity is never considered, and files tend to be highly segmented.

Under DOS 3.x, a stab was made at keeping things in one piece, with interesting implications for recovery. Large files, and especially files that are constantly undergoing change, such as database files, still tend to fragment rapidly and recurrently. But DOS 3.x tends to move things around on the disk without telling you, so there may be previous versions of a file in unallocated areas of the disk. That's worth knowing when all else fails and the only hope is to rebuild a file from scratch with raw data from the disk.

Seven in ten isn't a bad average in baseball, but when it comes to recovering deleted data it's bush league. Any failure rate is too high when the one file you wanted back is the one you didn't get. This stuff is valuable if only in terms of the time spent entering it into the computer. So, let's talk about the less than ideal situations.

When an UnDelete or UnErase program compares the old start address in the directory with the corresponding map entry in the FAT, it hopes to find a single, unallocated sequence that represents original file size or greater, in available storage. If that fails to be the case, the program usually presumes the file was fragmented. Some initial portion of the file is located, but the rest was stored elsewhere, and lacking any idea what the old FAT map looked like, quick recovery is out of the question.

Mace, and the latest editions of Norton and PC-Tools Deluxe, allow you to piece together a file manually. The procedure for recovering a fragmented file is one of searching, reviewing and saving. Most importantly, you should always try to *recover data to some other drive*. Never recover files to the same drive from which you're trying to retrieve them. The smaller the file, the higher the success rate.

Knowledge Required

CURE: As always, my first advice is to STOP! Take your hands off the keyboard, get a grip on the edge, and push yourself away from your desk.

You may want to get any oaths,

curses, or expletives out of your system right away. Prayer at this juncture is also often soothing, though it's not clear whether God understands computers better than mortals. Just don't hit any keys. (Don't hit *anything*; you may want two good hands before you're finished.)

Cure

Quick Undelete

PC-Tools may identify some files for "quick" Undeleting by placing a " " character next to the file extension. If MIRROR was installed, Undelete will use its backup copy of the FAT as a key to restoring the file, even if it was fragmented. This makes success highly probable and automatic.

Whether MIRROR was installed or not, check your files and immediately delete any that aren't recovered completely intact.

Undelete

This is part of the main program, PCTOOLS. From the main menu, press **F3** for the file handling menu. Choose by high-lighting whether to Undelete a file or directory, then press RETURN.

Use the arrow keys to high-light the directory where the deleted files used to be displayed, and press RETURN. Then use the arrow keys to high-light your file in the list. PC-Tools allows you to select any number of files at once for Undeleting. The first character is missing, because DOS replaced it with a sigma to denote erasure. You must replace it with some legitimate character. Normally it doesn't matter what that character is, unless you are working with accounting software or some other package that's religiously linked to a certain named file. DOS doesn't care. You can Undelete any data to any name, then rename later from DOS if that proves necessary.

When filling in the missing letter, the starting cluster (#CLU) is listed near the top. Write it down. If you go exploring you may need to come back to this spot on the disk.

The recovery menu gives you two ways of tracking down your data. Since there's no real penalty, you'll probably want to try "Automatic selection of clusters" first to see how lucky you are.

PC-Tools Undelete works by making up a new FAT chain as you select and order data. It's not modifying your disk—not until you say so. It's keeping track of which cluster goes where. When you tell it to "Save file" it creates a new set of FAT entries and fixes the missing character in the directory.

Escape to DOS and try loading the file into an application to see if it's all right. If not, you'll have to delete it and try manual recovery.

Typically, if you don't get what you want with the automatic recovery, you'll have to search for data. Find the first piece of your file by searching for

Cure

Cure

some key word, but before you add that cluster, press **End** and look at the end of what you're about to save. If it breaks in the middle of a word and you know what that word was, you can search for the missing piece next. Now add this cluster and go to the next.

Say the found fragment ended with "ho" and you know from context that this is the word "hotel." Search for the fragment "tel." You expect to find it at the start of another cluster. No other match counts. When you find "tel" go to the end again and note the missing fragment to search for before adding this cluster to the file. If there's no break in the last word, you'll have to guess at what must have come next.

I encourage you to be procedural about this. It takes less time in the long run, and PC-Tools doesn't let you back up to review.

I presume you're recovering text, or something with text in it, like a database or worksheet file. Since it's likely there have been a number of revisions, it is equally probable that the deleted areas of the disk contain more than one whole or fragmentary copy of the data. The differences may be subtle, so go slow. Remember, *you're not altering the disk*, you're telling PC-Tools what data on the disk to link up in the FAT and in what order.

When the "x of x clusters added to file" message indicates you've recovered everything, press **F3** to save the data as a file, escape to DOS, and try loading the file into an application to work on it.

If the file won't load, you'll have to delete it and start over. You may be missing something from the head or tail of the file.

Spreadsheet and database files in particular usually have "header" information preceding the first recognizable data. This often includes things you might recognize, such as the filename, a creation date, field definitions, and printer defaults. Similarly, there may be data following the last recognizable text, so make sure you don't throw away a few lines of information at the end, thinking you'll retype them; along with them, you may have left out important tables your program needs to interpret the data. You may have picked up and mixed in obsolete copies of the data alongside current copies. Try again and pay close attention to the splices, that is, the places where one cluster adjoins another.

Cure

File Not Listed

If you did some work after erasing the file, it's possible that DOS re-used the directory slot but didn't actually write over the file's data on the disk. This is likely under DOS major Version 3.x. Choose any file. For the most part, files don't "know" their own names, and DOS couldn't care less, so long as the name doesn't contain prohibited characters (.?*|\/<>). Recovery is that same as it was for fragmented files, a manual procedure. Simply search for the start of the file that interests you and begin there. You can rename the file after you've captured it.

Cure

Undeleting Directories

Directories, as I've said elsewhere, are simply files that contain directory information. With the exception of the root directory, they all begin with two special entries, . and .. and are easy to recognize.

Two things make Unerasing a directory different. The first piece must have . and .. entries. And all the other entries will show as deleted, the first character replaced with a sigma. That's because, of course, DOS forces you to delete everything before letting you remove the directory. If you use a search to find the directory entries, don't search for the whole filename; omit the first letter, or use a "?," which will match anything, including the sigma. Once recovered, the directory will still look empty from DOS's perspective. You'll have to Unerase the files one at a time.

Second, because DOS doesn't keep track of the size of a directory, there's no automatic way of knowing when it's fully recovered, except that the last piece usually (but not always) has some unused slots. It's up to you to deter-

Cure

mine that all the files in the directory are accounted for.

SUMMARY:

PC-Tools's Quick Undelete is accurate for fragmented files provided **MIRROR** runs periodically. Still, check your files afterwards to insure accuracy.

Normal Undelete involves identifying and piecing together clusters of data. It relies on your ability to make enough sense of the data to ensure an accurate sequence. Undelete takes care of actually reconstructing the File Allocation Table and directory entry based on the way you say things should look. This can be a trial and error process, but any data you can locate can be turned into a valid file.

dBASE File Is Lost

DIAGNOSIS:

A dBASE II, III, or III+ file was erased and couldn't be Unerased or Undeleted. Or the drive was formatted or suffered a low-level failure.

TOOLS REQUIRED:

You'll need dbFIX, listed in the back of the book. An expert might be able to use dSALVAGE, but it would be tedious; this is one place where dbFIX clearly outshines the competition.

KNOWLEDGE REQUIRED:

dBASE files consist of three parts, a header, records, and possibly memos. The header contains, among other things, field definitions for you records, such as FIRST, LAST, CITY, STATE, ZIP, DATE, etc., as well as the size and type of each field, record length, how many records are in the file and what version of dBASE was used to create the file. The format is unique, and dbFIX can find all the headers on any drive up to 512 megabytes, provided you can get a DOS prompt.

Records are the actual information you've stored in the database. They are all the same length and information in them must conform to certain rules, depending on the field types defined. Dates, for example, would always take the form 10/22/89.

Memos are notes attached to records. Recovery at this level is probably going to cost you any memos attached to the database, though the actual memo file can be recovered and re-entered.

CURE:

dbFIX will search any disk for all dBASE headers, then let you retrieve the data that belongs to it, even if no files or directories are visible. Once you find a header, you can match data to it with either dbFIX or dSALVAGE and determine if it belongs to that dBASE file.

If you can't find a header but you can identify your data, you can, with dbFIX, use the data to guess at the original header definition. You "paint" one field after another onto the data until a new header is defined, then set dbFIX to automatically hunt down every record on the disk that matches, even records stored in fragmented files.

SUMMARY:

For complete, automated recovery of lost dBASE files, dbFIX is unsurpassed. That's how I designed it. For quick repair of specific damage, dSALVAGE is best. That's how Paul Heiser designed it. In this case, dbFIX is more appropriate.

Since dBASE information is stored in ASCII format—English, more or less—it's likely you'll recognize some piece of your data. That's all that's really necessary to get your data off the affected disk.

You may recover extra records from old copies of the file, but you're certain

Summary

to get back at least all of your original information, provided it hasn't been destroyed or overwritten.

The manuals for dbFIX and dSALVAGE are comprehensive. In the future make more frequent backups.

dBASE Won't Let You Past a Certain Record, Though the File Is Much Longer and Contains Many More Records

DIAGNOSIS: An End-of-File mark has been imbedded in the middle of your dBASE file. This is a common occurrence.

TOOLS REQUIRED: You want Mace Utilities dbFIX or Comtech's dSALVAGE listed in the back of the book.

KNOWLEDGE REQUIRED: dBASE recovery is its own subject. Both of the salvage programs contain extensive explanations.

Text or Word Processing File Damaged or Lost

DIAGNOSIS: This can result from all sorts of disasters, ranging from accidental deletion to "invalid drive specification." The point is, you've lost data, primarily ASCII text (which may include database files) and other forms of recovery have been less than perfect.

TOOLS REQUIRED: Mace TextFIX or Norton's Text Search (TS).

KNOWLEDGE REQUIRED: ASCII (American Standard Code for Information Interchange) roughly defined, is the set of characters you can type on the keyboard, the alphabet, both upper and lowercase, numbers, punctuation marks, and a few special characters.

While they typically store other information, concerning format, typestyle, printer information as binary information, most word processors store all or most of their text in ASCII form. So do many database programs. This information is easy to recognize on sight and, once recovered, is relatively easy to import back into an application. Rare is the major program that doesn't allow ASCII import.

Some programs follow the WordStar convention and store some information in extended ASCII—what looks like Greek, and often is, substituted for the first character in most words. The results are eerie, but still decipherable.

There is another standard, EBCDIC, used by IBM mainframes and minis and DisplayWrite for the PC. This is unrecognizable from the DOS TYPE command, but can be deciphered by Mace TextFIX and Norton's Text Search.

Knowledge Required

Most programs also contain some ASCII text for error messages and help screens. Recovery involves locating the textual information in the midst of all the binary data on the disk and either splicing together the pieces to form a good file, or dumping every bit of text on the disk to an ASCII file and then editing it with a word processor or text editor back into it's original format. Mace TextFIX goes two steps further: It automates the splicing, and actually "understands" the special characteristics of several major word processors, and can retrieve their text files with format information intact.

CURE: *Recovering Lost or Damaged Files*

Mace Utilities offers you two possibilities. First, REMEDY will fix the file in cases where Abort Retry has got you stopped. You can look up that procedure under "Abort Retry Ignore." You can also specify or look up a file, active or deleted, and use TextFIX to search for and recover it. Norton Text Search will also let you specify and search for pieces of an active file, or other lost bits.

Cure

Splicing Lost ASCII Data Back Together

DOS stores data in chunks called clusters. There's no prescribed order to the chunks on the disk. While you're accustomed to seeing things in sequence, that's not necessarily the way they're ordered on the disk. The recovery situation is improved when you run a defragger, such as Mace Unfrag, Disk Optimizer, or Vopt. But retrieving data often still involves your finding and then declaring which piece goes where in the sequence. Usually this is a matter of searching for some key word or phrase you know must appear in the document you want, preferably at, or very near, the beginning.

The problem is there are likely to be multiple copies of the information you want stored on the disk. This results from the fact that DOS never erases data, only overwrites it when new data is added to the disk. Also, under DOS major Version 3.x, files move around on the disk without your knowing it, so DOS may place subsequent revisions of a file in numerous different places around the disk before it ever reuses a spot and overwrites what was there previously. Finally, most word processing and database programs create temporary files that also contain copies of some or all your data at some point.

The good news is you may have more than one chance of recovering some revision of the data you want, but you'll have to make sure you've got exactly the one you want. With both Mace TextFIX and Norton Text Search you can search the disk one match at a time. With Mace you can search the entire disk for all matches, and then review and compare them in a built-in editor to see which one you'd like. Additionally, with Mace once you've searched the disk for that first match, the program knows where the text is and what's binary data, so it never has to search the whole disk unproductively again. This can make the rest of the recovery very fast and efficient.

Once you've located the first piece of your file you want to examine the end of it. Very often this is part of a word or sentence. You want to identify in context what the rest of the word or sentence was and search for the missing fragment. For example, if the last sentence in the recovered cluster read "I was talking to Jon" and broke off, you'd recognize the missing part of the last word was the rest of "Jonathan." The sentence continued: "athan about his work habits." So, you'd search for some or all of that missing fragment. This would lead you (with luck) to the next missing piece.

You want the search text to be unique enough that it doesn't match all

Cure

over the place. Obviously, searching for the word or character string "the" is going to result in a stupendous number of matches, where "the blue flower" should be fairly unique. Of course, the longer the search string, the more effort the program makes to find a match and the longer the process. "The blue flower in the vase in the kitchen" is certainly a unique, but overly long fragment. Think before you search.

You may find the part you're looking imbedded-in, rather than at the start of, a cluster. This means you've located a piece of some version of the file that doesn't agree with the one you started with. You want the match that comes at the very head, to splice onto the very tale of what you've already accepted.

In Mace TextFIX you would actually see the new piece spliced onto the original, with a color change at the point where the two mated, so it's easy to see if the pieces match accurately. With Norton Text Search you would merely see the new piece and have to imagine what they look like together.

Recovery is a matter of repeating this process. You review the text you've located, to make certain it is exactly the piece you want and not something from an earlier revision, or a fragment from some other place in the document. You look at the splice point, where the new piece fits the already accepted pieces, then you tell the program you accept it, and move on.

When you get to the end you'll almost certainly see some junk. That's

Cure

because the document rarely fills the last cluster. What you see is whatever was stored there before your document was recorded (partially) over it. With Mace TextFIX, the last thing you'll want to do is mark the end of the file. This simply involves moving the cursor to the end of the recognizable text and pressing RETURN. With Norton Text Search you'll have to accept this junk for now and try to eliminate it with your word-processor.

Cure

Dumping the Disk

This means what it sounds like. The disk is scoured for identifiable text and this is then dumped into valid files on some other disk or series of disks as ASCII data—plain, raw text. It is then up to you to review and edit the files looking for what's important, then cutting and pasting blocks text back into their original sequence. If the disk has been recently defragged, this can be a quick and efficient way of getting text back. Bear in mind, you'll be losing all the format information, margins, spacing, fonts, bold, italics, etc. But the main text will be there, so you won't have to retype.

SUMMARY: When all else fails, you can always locate textual data with Mace TextFIX or Norton Text Search and reclaim it as a usable file. Mace offers some advantages in making the process faster and simpler, and works on disks to 512 megabytes capacity. Other than the disk size restrictions in the current Norton, both can accomplish the desired end result.

It's worth noting, your database files may be largely ASCII data (in dBASE, they are all ASCII), and so may your spreadsheet. You likely can retrieve them this way and reimport them into the database, or spreadsheet. If you are using dBASE, you'll find dbFIX in Mace more suited to the job.

Lotus 1-2-3 File Damaged or Lost

DIAGNOSIS:

This happens most often on floppy-based machines when disks are changed at the wrong moment, though other disk related problems can do you in.

TOOLS REQUIRED:

You want the Lotus recovery package RESCUE. The address and phone number are listed in the back of the book.

Chapter 3
Major Disasters

Problems

This section covers failures beyond the realm of human interference, though even here it's not the machines but a berserk piece of software that often leads to failure. While it's not always possible to tell, it's almost always possible to recover.

Your machine probably ran fine until you rebooted, or turned the power off. That's because most dramatic failures involve the Master Boot Record (MBR) and DOS only checks the MBR once, on power-up or warm reboot (Ctrl-Alt-Del). If the MBR is corrupted, or the area of the disk where it resides goes bad afterwards, you won't know it until reboot.

There are, of course, hardware failures, not all of them fatal. It's hard to tell at first. The steps that follow begin with the presumption that you won't have to open the machine to recover. They end with the opposite assumption, but are arranged so that if one recovery procedure doesn't produce results, you're in a good position to try the next. The degree of difficulty goes up but the possibility of complete recovery is there at almost all times.

You'll need a DOS system diskette in drive A: to boot the machine. If you use the original DOS diskette, the next thing you'll need to do is FORMAT a blank diskette with the /s (system) option. Then put the original DOS diskette back in a safe place.

Quick Cure

If you are confident that you have a complete current backup of all your data to restore, you can always reinitialize the disk with a low-level format, FDISK and DOS format.

Before you do that, you should read the first three diagnoses; they might resolve your problem faster and easier than restoring from backups. In any case, you should read the section of this book on initializing your hard disk, under Staying Out of Trouble.

The Machine Worked Fine When You Turned It Off the Night Before but Was Dead on Arrival in the Morning

DIAGNOSIS: Your drive may be cold. Is the temperature constant where the machine is located? Is the heat off or lowered at night? If so, it's possible that your machine was running hot at the end of the day, and is now stone cold.

TOOLS REQUIRED: Patience and a little luck.

KNOWLEDGE REQUIRED: Accurate positioning of the read/write heads over the data tracks is critical to your disk. They're sensitive to thermal cycling, the dramatic swings in the amount of heat they're subjected to. It's possible that your machine simply can't position the cold disk mechanism correctly. Warming things up to where they were when you left at the end of the day might help.

CURE: Leave the machine on for an hour or so. I know, it won't recognize C:, but the hard disk is always running when the power is on. It will eventually warm up. After an hour, turn the machine off, then on again. If you're

Cure

lucky, the machine will come up normally.

Back up your data and run a low-level diagnostic program, such as HTEST. It may be necessary to do a fresh, low-level format of your disk while the machine is running at normal operating temperature.

Also, check the back of your machine. Make sure all the metal plates are in place—the silver ones that block slots for internal cards. Your computer won't cool properly with those plates missing, so put them back whenever you remove an internal card. If you've lost them, use electrician's tape or duct tape to block the openings.

An AT-Style Machine Won't Boot, or Recognize Drive C:

DIAGNOSIS: On an AT your SETUP information may be bad, due to a dying battery or an errant program. Often the computer will prompt you when this information is bad, but not always. The "drive type" information may be incorrect without the computer knowing it—except that it won't boot up.

TOOLS REQUIRED: SETUP.EXE or the setup disk that came with your machine. If you're not sure, contact your trusty local dealer or the manufacturer of your machine.

KNOWLEDGE REQUIRED: On an AT the hardware configuration is stored in 32 bytes of memory that run off a battery that's usually stuck to the inside back of the machine next to the power supply, that is, next to the chrome cage with all the nasty warning stickers on it.

If that battery fails, you should get a message to run SETUP. But it doesn't always happen that way. Also, programs have been known to clobber the information the battery is backing up—specifically, what type hard disk is installed—and it needs to be reset correctly.

Note: SETUP from one brand of AT

Knowledge Required

CURE: You'll have to run the program
SETUP.EXE that came with your machine. You also may need to open the
machine to determine the drive type
(or call the dealer who sold it to you).
There is usually a prominent number
on a sticker, or stamped on the front or
top of the hard disk.

After SETUP the machine reboots. It
should come up normally. If not, run
setup again to see if the information
you just put in is unchanged. If it looks
bad, replace the battery and run
SETUP again. If the information looks
good, and you are certain the drive
type is correct, go to the next section.

SUMMARY: Some hard disk failures on AT-class
machines are the result of incorrect
setup information due to a failing battery or an errant program altering the
setup information. Running SETUP to
correct the "drive type" and/or replacing the battery will cure this problem.

may not work right on another. IBM
won't handle Compaq, for example.

"Invalid Drive Specification" Message Appears

**Your disk was partitioned using third-party software such as VFea-
ture, Speedstor, or Disk Manager.**

DIAGNOSIS: Your disk may have been partitioned
originally with a special program and
that file was either erased inadver-
tently or corrupted. Or the CON-
FIG.SYS file on the boot drive was
erased or corrupted.

TOOLS REQUIRED: You'll need a fresh copy of the original
software, preferably the disk used to
install it on your machine. You'll probably need the manual for that software
handy as well.

KNOWLEDGE REQUIRED: Programs like these usually come in
the form of installable device drivers—
the device to be driven, in this case,
being your hard disk.
There would have been a file, called
CONFIG.SYS in the root directory of
the boot drive—typically drive C:, and
it would have contained a statement
like:

device = *something*.sys

where *something* is the name of the
partitioning software.

If the device driver file or the CON-FIG.SYS file is either erased or corrupted, the disk won't be initialized when you turn the power on, and DOS will claim it isn't there.

CURE: You'll need to get a fresh copy of the driver software off the disk used to install it. Not just any copy, please. These programs configure the driver during installation to your machine. Some versions of VFeature actually code it to work only with a specific machine. So, if it's at all realistic, take the time to dig out the diskette that was actually in this machine when the installation took place.

Copy that driver onto the diskette you are using to boot the machine. Consult the manual for the software you were using about special parameters. If you have the original installation diskette, it's doubtful special parameters will be needed. Device drivers used to create extra partitions (drives D: E: F: ...) may, however, take optional parameters.

You'll need to create a new CON-FIG.SYS file on the floppy disk you're using to boot the machine. Assuming you boot from the A: drive, type the following at the command line:

COPY CON CONFIG.SYS and press RETURN
DEVICE = *something*, where *something* is the driver name.

press RETURN

press F6 function key

press RETURN

What we've done here is copy from the CONsole (your screen) to the file CONFIG.SYS. The F6 key places a control Z (^Z) or End-of-File marker, on the screen, alerting the operating system that you are done and want to write the file to disk.

Type DIR A: and press RETURN to do a directory of A: and you should see a CONFIG.SYS file listed. Now press Ctrl-Alt-Del, or turn your machine off and on, to reboot, and the missing drive(s) should reappear.

Cure

If this works, be sure to copy the device driver from the floppy to the C: drive. Also, be certain there is a CONFIG.SYS file in the root directory of C:.

Type DIR C:\CONFIG.SYS and press RETURN.

If you do see a listing, type TYPE C:\CONFIG.SYS and press RETURN.

This will display the contents of the file. If it doesn't, or there is no device = statement for your disk driver, you'll need to copy the CONFIG.SYS from the floppy in A: to the root directory of C:.

SUMMARY:

Disks configured with third-party device drivers will vanish if those device driver files are erased or corrupted. You can recover by reconfiguring a floppy system disk with the original

Summary

driver, rebooting from A:, then copying the device driver to C:.

You'd be well advised to get Compaq DOS 3.32 or DOS 4.0, which support multiple partitions up to 512 megabytes. They help create a more stable computing environment, where this problem doesn't exist.

"Invalid Drive Specification" or Machine Won't Recognize the C: Drive

DIAGNOSIS:
The Master Boot Record (MBR) at the very beginning of your disk is incorrect or corrupt, or simply not activated.

TOOLS REQUIRED:
You may get by with just a DOS system diskette and FDISK.COM, if the problem is simply a deactivated DOS partition. Depending on the extent of the trouble, you may also need a low-level hard disk formatter—some machines come with one built-in.

I will be recommending and talking about Htest/Hformat, which I publish, and its companion programs XFDISK and GETSEC, because they're the only software tools currently available that make recovery from this situation safe and reasonably certain.

Bear in mind, until the day Marc Kolod and I found each other in 1986, bailing out a dead disk at Boeing, each of us was telling people in this situation there was a high probability they wouldn't get anything back. Together, we realized, with Hformat, GETSEC, and Mace UnFormat, we had the power to help people recover substantially from any situation short of permanent

Tools Required

physical damage to the disk or data. While Norton and Central Point Software have since duplicated some of the features of Mace, there are, as of this writing, no alternatives to Htest/Hformat that I know of.

KNOWLEDGE REQUIRED:

We may need to fix the MBR. The MBR is located in the absolute top, outside track of the physical drive. It tells the computer what Operating System is active (you can have more than one— UNIX for instance), what part of the disk it occupies, and where, precisely, more information can be found for booting that Operating System.

The MBR is created by FDISK prior to DOS FORMAT, but some versions of FDISK don't automatically activate the DOS partition when they create it, leaving the appearance that nothing has happened and the drive's not there.

QUICK CURE:

If you're in a hurry, and the partition is listed as "Active" by FDISK, and Mace, Norton Advanced, or PC-Tools Deluxe was installed before this happened, you could FDISK and then recover as if from an accidental FORMAT. Each of the three programs creates a copy of most of the information FDISK destroys. Note: I said most, not all. Also, the backup file may not be current, and you could lose some recent work. So, think of them as fall-

Quick Cure

back positions. If all else fails and either of the three were installed, you can get most of your data back by turning to the section Recovering As If From an Accidental FORMAT.

CURE: I'll assume you're on the A: drive and have the DOS program FDISK.COM on the diskette in A:.

We're going to examine some information, but you won't be modifying anything right now. Type FDISK and press RETURN. Press 4 to view disk parameters.

FDISK will try to read the MBR from the first sector on the disk. If it can't, you'll need to do a low-level format of that sector. Skip to the diagnostic Invalid Drive Specification. FDISK Reports Errors.

You may see a message something like, "No partitions defined". If so, skip the next two paragraphs.

If information about starting and ending cylinders is displayed, look at the category headed "Active Partition." There should be an "A" for "Active" opposite the first partition (which should be of type "DOS").

If there is a "N" for "Not active" instead, that's your problem. You need to make DOS active. This is a simple and harmless operation. First Press <Esc> to return to the main menu, then press the key for the option labeled "Change active partition". FDISK will ask you what partition you want to make active. Press the number of the partition labeled "DOS", to indicate it should be made active. Then quit FDISK and reboot the machine. All should be well. If no partitions are defined, the MBR is defunct, and must be recreated.

Unfortunately, FDISK erases the FAT's and root directory at the same time it creates the MBR. C: would come back, but it would appear empty—not what we want. For disks prepared with DOS major Version 3.x, FDISK has the added disadvantage of writing into the first part of the data area to make certain it's error free for the DOS system files.

Cure

Odds are you're reading this because you weren't protected in any way. You're going to need Htest/Hformat, written by Marc Kolod and published by me. If and when there are alternatives, I'll recommend them. For now, the Htest package has what you need: XFDISK.

XFDISK works just like DOS FDISK, except that it doesn't touch anything other than the MBR. With XFDISK you can redefine the partition, reboot, and your disk will be just as it was.

SUMMARY:

You can start over from scratch, FDISKing and running DOS FORMAT. You can restore from backups if you have them. If Mace, Norton Advanced, or PC-Tools Deluxe were in-

Summary

stalled, you can FDISK, then restore asif from an accidental FORMAT and get substantial recovery. Or you can get the Htest software and use its XFDISK utility to completely recover. There are no other alternatives.

FDISK Reports an Error Reading the Disk Whenever You Attempt to View Partition Information or Perform Any Other FDISK Operation

Mace, Norton Advanced, or PC-Tools Deluxe were *not* installed.

DIAGNOSIS:

The Master Boot Record (MBR) at the very beginning of your disk is unreadable. Physical format information has been corrupted. At a minimum, the entire first track on the disk will have to be reformatted.

TOOLS REQUIRED:

You need a low-level hard disk formatter—some machines come with one built-in. I'll be talking about Hformat, written by Marc Kolod and published by me, as well as it's companion programs XFDISK and GETSEC, because they're the only software tools currently available that make recovery from this situation safe and reasonably certain. IBM's Advanced Diagnostics won't work. The format program wipes out the disk from back to front, leaving you with nothing to recover.

KNOWLEDGE REQUIRED:

We need to fix the formatting information on the first track of the disk, then recreate the MBR. The MBR is located in the absolute top, outside track of the physical drive. It tells the computer what Operating System is active, what part of the disk it occupies, and where, precisely, more information can be found for booting that Operating System. The MBR is created by FDISK, prior to DOS FORMAT.

For disks prepared with FDISK and FORMAT under PC- or MS-DOS major Version 2.x, the MBR occupies the first sector, or 512 bytes, on the disk. The DOS boot record for the C: partition begins in the very next sector, typically followed by two copies of the File Allocation Table (FAT), the root directory, and then any files and subdirectories.

For disks FDISKed and FORMATted under DOS major Version 3.x, the MBR takes up the entire first track— usually 17 sectors. The DOS boot record, FATs, root directory, and data begin on the next track, the one recorded on the bottom side of the topmost platter.

Regardless of whose software you use, all low-level format programs format at least one whole track at a time, not single sectors. They replace any data recorded on the disk with a fill pattern. You can see, for disks formatted under DOS major Version 2, this poses a problem: to cure the first sector we must wipe out sixteen sectors of vital information. With DOS major Version 3 we are in better shape; the MBR occupies the whole first track.

If you have a low-level format program, chances are it doesn't let you control what tracks you want to format; it wants to do the whole disk. IBM's Advanced Diagnostics wants to do it back to front. You can, of course, start the low level-format of your disk and then immediately kill the power and hope you didn't go too far; this will save you the price of special software—and cost you some or all your data.

Hformat is recommended because it's the most flexible in this respect. You can select a specific track and format just it, preserving the data you don't want to lose. The Htest/Hformat package also includes GETSEC and PUT-SEC, two programs that read and write to disks that DOS can't access. They help resolve what to do on a DOS 2 disk. We can save the good data in those sixteen sectors, format the track, then lay the data back down. You'll also see as we go along, because the damage is often more extensive than just the first track, GETSEC and PUT-SEC can become invaluable.

Until 1986, I was telling people in this situation there was a high probability they wouldn't get everything back. I, along with Marc Kolod, realized, with Hformat, GETSEC and Mace UnFormat, we had the power to help people recover substantially from any situation short of permanent physical damage to the disk or data. While Norton and Central Point Software have

Knowledge Required

Knowledge Required

QUICK CURE:

since duplicated some of the features of Mace, there are, as of this writing, no alternatives to Htest/Hformat that I know of.

I don't recommend it, but if you're too impatient or too poor to do it right, you can proceed as follows, provided you have a low-level format program and plan to buy immediately, Mace Utilities, or PC-Tools Deluxe. (If you already own one of them, or Norton Advanced, and they were installed, go to the next diagnostic, Invalid Drive Specification. Mace, Norton Advanced, or PC-Tools Deluxe was installed.)

To do a partial recovery, run the low-level formatter and immediately kill the power. That is, tell it to go ahead and the moment you hit RETURN, pull the plug, or hit the big red switch on the side or back of the machine. This should repair the defective track. If not, you may have to repeat the process and take a deep breath between activating the formatter and killing the power.

Then FDISK, and run DOS FORMAT (provided it's not Compaq Version 3.2 or earlier, or ATT 3.1 or earlier, which are lethal. For them substitute PC-DOS Format or MACE Format-H). Then run Mace UnFormat or PC-Tools Deluxe format recovery.

You're going to lose some vital data doing things this way. Subdirectory files that weren't fragmented, that is,

Quick Cure

stored in more than one physical piece on the disk, will be recovered.

Warning: If you go for the quick cure, you can't go back and do it right.

CURE:

First, we need to do a low-level format of the corrupted track. This isn't the same as a DOS FORMAT, which on a hard disk is almost always "logical." This is a simple verification. Low-level formatters come either as a separate diagnostic disk, or third party software, such as Htest/Hformat, or built into some third-party hard disk controller cards.

To determine if your machine has a low-level format program built-in, you'll need a copy of DEBUG.COM or DEBUG.EXE in the A: drive. From the A> prompt:

Type DEBUG and press RETURN.

Type G=C800:5 and press RETURN.

If the format program appears, **do nothing!** Skip the next paragraph.

If nothing happens immediately, you don't have a built-in low-level formatter. You'll have to reboot your machine by pressing Ctrl-Alt-Del, or possibly by turning the power off and on. You'll need third party software, such as Htest/Hformat.

The recommended procedure at this point is to obtain the Htest/Hformat package listed in the back of the book

Cure

and use GETSEC to save all the data on the first five cylinders of the disk. If you do this, you leave yourself with the best chance of 100 percent recovery, no matter what difficulties are encountered. If you don't use GETSEC, some data loss is inevitable, and any mistake you make beyond this point could be irreversible.

If you have an RLL disk controller—one that packs 50 percent or more data, say 30 megabytes on a 20 megabyte disk—turn to the diagnostic section, RLL Disk No Longer Recognized.

If your disk was formatted with DOS major Version 2.x, as I pointed out above, we have an immediate dilemma: the Master Boot Record occupies only one sector. The balance of the first track is devoted to DOS boot, FAT, and possible root directory information.

If you use GETSEC, note any reported errors. We already know there are errors on head 0, track 0, but make a note of any errors beyond that point. It may be necessary to low-level format those areas as well.

You can proceed with Hformat (or its equivalent on a DOS major Version 3 formatted disk) resetting the defaults to format head 0, track 0. Set the repeat value to 1. If there is a physical flaw in track zero, we do *not* want to find it. We want just one good take, so we can continue for the moment.

If you have some low-level format program other than HFORMAT that lets you control the track to be fixed,

Cure

use it to format head 0, track 0. Note, however, for disks formatted under DOS major Version 2, you are essentially placing yourself in the Quick Cure mode beyond this point. Vital data will be destroyed, and you'll need Mace or PC-Tools Deluxe to finish. Go to the Quick Cure section of this diagnostic.

If you elect for your own good reasons to play the BIG RED SWITCH game with an unknown low-level formatter, go back and read the Quick Cure section of this diagnostic.

If you got this far, I assume you have HFORMAT, (or its equivalent and a DOS major Version 3 formatted disk). You want to run it with the /NV parameter on the command line for "No Verify". You'll want to reset the default parameters to format starting and ending head 0, track or cylinder 0. Set the repeat count to 1. We want one good take. If the first track is defective, you don't want to know about it. In fact, pray that it isn't, or DOS will never recognize the drive, though we would still have one final shot at recovery.

Low-level format completed? Run FDISK or XFDISK again, option 4, "View disk parameters". If you get an error instead—no point denying it— that's not good news. It means the format information didn't take. If you're using HFORMAT, be sure to enter HFORMAT /NV on the command line—meaning "No Verify". Check to be sure you're formatting, starting and ending at head 0, track or cylinder 0.

Cure

We're looking for the "No partitions defined" message. That's our signal for initial success. If you can't get past the error message, you still have one good chance. Turn to the diagnostic titled Track 0 Low-Level Format Failed.

If you don't have XFDISK and GET-SEC, you're in a Quick Cure situation. Refer back to Quick Cure at the head of this diagnostic.

On a disk originally formatted with DOS major Version 2 we've wiped out some vital information while formatting track 0. You'll need to use GET-SEC's companion program, PUTSEC, to restore the data you saved. But you only want to restore head 0, track 0 at this juncture, not all five cylinders.

Our next step is to redefine the lost partition information in the Master Boot Record. The main menu of XFDISK contains an option titled "Define DOS partition". Select it. Most likely your C: drive started at cylinder 0 and you used the entire disk for DOS. If not, you'll have to supply the best guess.

With XFDISK there's no penalty for mistakes, other than time spent trying new combinations if the first guess doesn't work. When DOS FDISK runs, it tries to verify that the vital areas of the disk are error free. In the process, it not only reconstructs a Master Boot Record, it also wipes out the FATs, root directory, and some data on the partition being defined. XFDISK doesn't; it merely recreates the MBR.

After XFDISK has defined the MBR,

it prompts you to press a key to reboot. Open the A: drive door and press ES-Cape.

The machine should reboot from C: as if nothing had ever happened. Run the DOS program CHKDSK. If it reports no error, congratulations! Now, make an immediate backup of all your data—at the very least, copy all your valuable files to diskette or to some other physical drive or Bernoulli cartridge. You may have suffered one-time failure due to unknown hardware, software, or environmental events. Then again, you may have a major problem lurking. Read the section of this book titled Staying Out of Trouble.

If the machine didn't reboot from C:, or CHKDSK reported errors, relax. Close the A: drive door, reboot the machine from the DOS floppy.

Let's review the possibilities:

The partition may be there, but still be marked "Not active." Run XFDISK or FDISK selection 4, "View partition information." The "Status" column should show "A" for "Active" next to the DOS partition. If it shows "N," then you'll need to select from the main menu the "Change active partition" option and make the DOS partition "Active". Open the A: drive door, press ES-Cape and the machine should reboot from C:. Run CHKDSK. If no errors are reported, backup immediately and read the section Staying Out of Trouble.

Cure

Track 0 may be too weak to hold format information. XFDISK appeared to work, but each time you reboot you're right back where you started. Got to the diagnostic titled Track 0 Low-Level Format Failed.

C: is there but CHKDSK reports errors. On a disk originally formatted with DOS major Version 2 we wiped out some vital information while formatting track 0. You should already have restored track 0 with companion program, PUTSEC. If not, do that now. Then run XFDISK again, define a partition, reboot, run CHKDSK again, and all should be well.

Cure

CHKDSK or DOS persist in reporting errors. It's likely that the disk was screwed up beyond the first track. You probably noted these errors when you ran GETSEC. Reformatting track zero usually makes these errors go away. In this case, we weren't so lucky. But that's why we saved five cylinders of data at the outset, and noted the errors.

If your machine was opened for any reason just before all this trouble came upon it, or was moved, dropped, or had coffee spilled into its cooling slots, you should consider opening it now. Check all the cards. It wouldn't be a bad idea to pull them and put them back in. Check all the cables. I know, you didn't touch any cables, but check them anyway, both ends, where they connect to the card and to the disk.

It's possible that you have a bad disk controller card. If it's not out of the question, you might consider swapping controller cards with another machine, a friend, or your faithful local dealer. Because from here on in 100 percent recovery is out the window.

If nothing else works, you'll have to low-level format all the tracks on all the heads that reported errors, from cylinder 0 to cylinder 4 (for a total of 5). This is the area DOS uses for system information. You should PUTSEC again afterwards, XFDISK and reboot. Check for your most valuable files. Run CHKDSK, but don't be intimidated by errors. If you can copy off your most valuable files, do it now. Check their integrity. Some things are just not going to look right. When you've got everything you can get at, stop and turn to the section on Recovering From Accidental FORMAT. MACE, and more recently PC-Tools Deluxe, have the power to reconstruct the DOS system areas from data elsewhere on the disk, which describes the situation you are in: good data, bad FATs and root directory.

Cure

SUMMARY:

You can start over from scratch, FDISKing and running DOS FOR-MAT. You can restore from backups, if you have them. If Mace, Norton Advanced, or PC-Tools Deluxe were installed, you can FDISK, then restore as

Summary

if from an accidental FORMAT and get substantial recovery. Or you can get the H/test software and use its XFDISK and GETSEC utilities to completely recover. There are no other alternatives I now of.

"Invalid Drive Specification" Message

FDISK reports an error reading the disk whenever you attempt to view partition information, or perform any other FDISK operation. **Mace, Norton Advanced, or PC-Tools Deluxe** *was* **installed.**

DIAGNOSIS: The Master Boot Record (MBR) at the very beginning of your disk is unreadable. Physical format information has been corrupted. At a minimum, the entire first track on the disk will have to be reformatted.

The good news is, you had installed a program that duplicates most of this information in another place on the disk. All but your most recent work before the disk went dead can be restored.

For a chance at 100 percent restoration, you should follow the previous section, as if no backup information existed. If that fails, you can always try these procedures next.

TOOLS REQUIRED: The DOS program FDISK.COM will be needed for reestablishing the MBR.

You also need a low-level hard disk formatter to fix track 0. Some machines come with one built-in. I'll be talking about Hformat, written by Marc Kolod and published by me, as well as its companion programs XFDISK and GETSEC, because they're the only software tools currently available that make recovery from this situation safe and reasonably certain.

Until 1986, Marc Kolod and I were both telling people in this situation there was a high probability they wouldn't get everything back. Together, we realized, with Hformat, GETSEC and Mace UnFormat, we had the power to help people recover substantially from any situation short of permanent physical damage to the disk or data. While Norton and Central Point Software have since duplicated some of the features of Mace, there are, as of this writing, no alternatives to Htest/Hformat that I know of. IBM's Advanced Diagnostics won't work—the format program wipes out the disk from back to front, leaving you with nothing to recover.

Tools Required

You already had Mace, Norton Advanced, or PC-Tools Deluxe installed, correct? With them, you can restore as a last step as if from an accidental FORMAT.

KNOWLEDGE REQUIRED:

We need to fix the formatting information on the first track of the disk, then recreate the Master Boot Record (MBR).

The MBR is located in the absolute top, outside track of the physical drive. It tells the computer what Operating System is active, what part of the disk it occupies, and where, precisely, more information can be found for booting that Operating System.

The MBR is created by FDISK, prior to DOS FORMAT. For disks prepared with FDISK and FORMAT under PC- or MS-DOS major Version 2.x, the MBR occupies the first sector, or 512 bytes, on the disk. The DOS boot record for the C: partition begins in the very next sector, typically followed by two copies of the File Allocation Table (FAT), the root directory, and then any files and subdirectories.

For disks FDISKed and FORMATted under DOS major Version 3.x, the MBR takes up the entire first track— usually 17 sectors. The DOS boot record, FATs, root directory, and data begin on the next track, the one recorded on the bottom side of the top-most platter.

Knowledge Required

Regardless of whose software you use, all low-level format programs format at least one whole track at a time, not single sectors. They replace any data recorded on the disk with a fill pattern. You can see, for disks format-ted under DOS major Version 2, this poses a problem: to cure the first sector we must wipe-out sixteen sectors of vital information. With DOS major Version 3 we are in better shape; the MBR occupies the whole first track.

With Mace, Norton Advanced, or PC-Tools Deluxe installed, at least one copy or more of the critical FAT and root directory information has been made somewhere on drive C:. Once we get DOS to recognize C:, we can restore that information.

If you have a low-level format program, chances are it doesn't let you control what tracks you want to format; it wants to do the whole disk. IBM's Advanced Diagnostics wants to do it back to front. You can, of course, start the low level-format of your disk and then immediately kill the power and hope you didn't go too far; this will save you the price of special software—and cost you some or all your data.

Hformat is recommended because it's the most flexible in this respect. You can select a specific track and format just it, preserving the data you don't want to lose. The Htest/Hformat package also includes GETSEC and PUT-SEC, two programs that read and write to disks that DOS can't access. They help resolve what to do on a DOS 2 disk. We can save the good data in those sixteen sectors, format the track, then lay the data back down.

You'll also see as we go along, because the damage is often more extensive than just the first track, GETSEC and PUTSEC can become invaluable.

Knowledge Required

CURE: First, we need to do a low-level format of the corrupted track. This isn't the same as a DOS FORMAT, which, on a hard disk is almost always "logical". This is a simple verification. Low-level formatters come either as a separate diagnostic disk, or third party software, such as Htest/Hformat, or built into some third-party hard disk controller cards.

To determine if your machine has a

low-level format program built-in, you'll need a copy of DEBUG.COM or DEBUG.EXE in the A: drive. From the A> prompt:

Type DEBUG and press RETURN.

Type G = C800:5 and press RETURN.

If the format program appears, **do nothing!** Skip the next paragraph.

If nothing happens immediately, you don't have a built-in low-level formatter. You'll have to reboot your machine by pressing Ctrl-Alt-Del, or possibly by turning the power off and on. You'll need third party software, such as Htest/Hformat.

Cure

If you have an RLL disk controller—one that packs 50 percent or more data, say 30 megabytes on a 20 megabyte disk—turn to the diagnostic section RLL Disk No Longer Recognized.

If your disk was formatted with DOS major Version 2.x, as I pointed out above, we have an immediate dilemma: the Master Boot Record occupies only one sector. The balance of the first track is devoted to DOS boot, FAT, and possible root directory information.

You can proceed with Hformat (or its equivalent on a DOS major Version 3 formatted disk) resetting the defaults to format head 0, track 0. Set the repeat value to 1. If there is a physical flaw in track zero, we do *not* want to find it. We want just one good take, so we can continue for the moment.

If you have some low level format program other than HFORMAT that lets you control the track to be fixed, use it to format head 0, track 0. If you elect to risk it, you can play the BIG RED SWITCH game with an unknown low-level formatter. Here's what you do: set the format program ready to begin at the next keystroke. Poise one finger over the key that starts it, poise another finger on the master power switch (alternately, get a good grip on the power cord). Ready? Press the starting key and push (pull) with the other hand, killing the power.

You'll probably format more than one track, but there'll be a backup of roughly the first four cylinders of data.

Cure

If you're not a high-roller, I assume you have HFORMAT (or its equivalent and a DOS major Version 3 formatted disk). You want to run it with the /NV parameter on the command line—for "No Verify". You'll want to reset the default parameters to format starting and ending head 0, track or cylinder 0. Set the repeat count to 1. We want one good take. If the first track is defective, you don't want to know about it. In fact, pray that it isn't, or DOS will never recognize the drive, though we would still have one final shot at recovery.

Low-level format completed? Run FDISK or XFDISK again, option 4, "View disk parameters." If you get an error instead—no point denying it— that's not good news. It means the format information didn't take. If you're

Cure

using HFORMAT, be sure to enter HFORMAT /NV on the command line—meaning "No Verify." Check to be sure you're formatting, starting and ending at head 0, track or cylinder 0.

We're looking for the "No partitions defined" message. That's our signal for initial success. If you can't get past the error message, you still have one good chance. Turn to the diagnostic titled Track 0 Low-Level Format Failed.

If you don't have XFDISK you're going to loose some data, possibly the exact thing you want. FDISK not only clears out the FATs and root directory, it erases the first part of the data space, checking for a safe landing spot for the DOS system files. Alas, it goes a bit farther than strictly necessary and will clobber whatever came first or second on the disk after COM-MAND.COM. If the first thing you did when setting up the disk was create a subdirectory—no doubt your favorite one—it'll get wiped out. The good news is, CHKDSK/F will recover the files if you tell it "yes," to convert lost chains to files. But they'll all be called FI-LExxxx.CHK and you'll have to puzzle out their true identities. Also the sizes will be rounded off to the nearest clus-ter, which means some of them might not load correctly into your spread-sheet or word-processor. I know, you feel lucky. FDISK and pray.

Our next step is to redefine the lost partition information in the Master Boot Record. The main menu of XFDISK contains an option titled "De-

Cure

fine DOS partition". Select it. Most likely your C: drive started at cylinder 0 and you used the entire disk for DOS. If not, you will have to supply the best guess.

With XFDISK there's no penalty for mistakes, other than time spent trying new combinations if the first guess doesn't work. When DOS FDISK runs it tries to verify that the vital areas of the disk are error free. In the process, it not only reconstructs a Master Boot Record, it also wipes out the FATs, root directory, and some data on the partition being defined. XFDISK doesn't; it merely recreates the MBR.

After XFDISK has defined the MBR, it prompts you to press a key to reboot. Open the A: drive door and press ESCape.

The machine *may* reboot from C: as if nothing had ever happened. Run the DOS program CHKDSK. If it reports no error, congratulations! Now, make an immediate backup of all your data—at the very least, copy all your valuable files to diskette or to some other physical drive or Bernoulli cartridge. You may have suffered one-time failure due to unknown hardware, software, or environmental events. Then again, you may have a major problem lurking. Read the section of this book titled Staying Out of Trouble.

If the machine didn't reboot from C:, or CHKDSK reported errors, relax. Close the A: drive door, reboot the machine from the DOS floppy.

Get out your copy of Mace, Norton

Advanced, or PC-Tools Deluxe. With
Mace you want to run UnFormat and
answer "yes" when it asks if Mace was
installed. Norton wants FR (Format
Recovery). PC-Tools Deluxe wants the
UnFormat option.

All three restore the vital DOS system areas. If they sailed to completion
without errors, reboot the machine and
have a look at C:. All should be well,
with the exception of files and directories created or modified since the last
backup was made, usually the last
time the power was turned on, or the
machine rebooted with Ctrl-Alt-Del,
before disaster struck.

Run the DOS program CHKDSK.
Again, any errors should be restricted
to recent work. Load vital files and
check them for completeness. Now
back everything up, or at least copy vital files to some other place.

If restoration failed and C: is still invisible, let's review the possibilities.

*The partition may be there, but still
be marked "Not active."* Run
XFDISK or FDISK selection 4,
"View partition information." The
"Status" column should show "A" for
"Active" next to the DOS partition.
If it shows "N", then you'll need to
select from the main menu the
"Change active partition" option and
make the DOS partition "Active".
Open the A; drive door, press ES-
Cape and the machine should reboot
from C:. Run CHKDSK. If no errors
are reported, backup immediately

Cure

and read the section Staying Out of Trouble.

Track 0 may be too weak to hold format information. XFDISK appeared to work, but each time you reboot you're right back where you started. Got to the diagnostic titled Track 0 Low-Level Format Failed.

CHKDSK or DOS persist in reporting errors. It's likely that the disk was screwed up beyond the first track. Reformatting track zero usually makes these errors go away. In this case, we weren't so lucky.

Cure

If your machine was opened for any reason just before all this trouble came upon it, or was moved, dropped, or had coffee spilled into its cooling slots, you should consider opening it now. Check all the cards. It wouldn't be a bad idea to pull them and put them back in. Check all the cables. I know, you didn't touch any cables, but check them anyway, both ends, where they connect to the card and to the disk.

It's possible that you have a bad disk controller card. If it's not out of the question, you might consider swapping controller cards with another machine, a friend, or your faithful local dealer.

If nothing else works, you'll have to low-level format all the tracks on all the heads that reported errors, from cylinder 0 to cylinder 4 (for a total of 5). This is the area DOS uses for system information. XFDISK or FDISK and reboot. Restore again with Mace,

Norton or PC-Tools and check for your most valuable files. Run CHKDSK, but don't be intimidated by errors. If you can copy off your most valuable files, do it now. Check their integrity. Some things are just not going to look right.

Cure

If all else fails, stop and turn to the section on Recovering From Accidental FORMAT. Mace, and more recently PC-Tools Deluxe, have the power to reconstruct the DOS system areas from data elsewhere on the disk, which describes the situation you are in: good data, bad FATs and root directory.

SUMMARY:

You can start over from scratch, FDISKing and running DOS FOR-MAT. You can restore from backups if you have them. If Mace, Norton Advanced, or PC-Tools Deluxe were installed, you can FDISK, then restore as if from an accidental FORMAT and get substantial recovery. Or you can get the Htest software and use its XFDISK and GETSEC utilities to completely recover.

"Invalid Drive Specification" Message. RLL Disk No Longer Recognized

FDISK reports an error reading the disk whenever you attempt to view partition information, or perform any other FDISK operation. **Mace, Norton Advanced, or PC-Tools Deluxe were *not* installed.**

DIAGNOSIS: If you have an RLL disk controller, one that packs 50 percent or more data (say 30 megabytes on a 20 megabyte disk) you *must* use GETSEC, as we're going to be forced to use a special, low-level formatter against the disk and the BIG RED SWITCH that turns the computer on and off will be our only control over the process.

This category includes many "hard disks on a card", especially drive cards with 30 megabytes or more capacity, and *all* Plus Development HardCards.

The Master Boot Record (MBR) at the very beginning of your disk is unreadable. Physical format information has been corrupted, and on most RLL type drives this format information is doubly peculiar. At a minimum, the entire first track on the disk will have to be reformatted with the controller card manufacturer's low-level format program.

TOOLS REQUIRED:

You need a low-level hard disk formatter (some RLL controllers come with one built-in). I'll also be talking about Hformat, written by Marc Kolod and published by me, as well as its companion programs XFDISK and GETSEC, but you'll still need a format program from your controller card's manufacturer because they're all different and Hformat won't do the job completely. IBM's Advanced Diagnostics won't work. The format program wipes out the disk from back to front, leaving you with nothing to recover.

KNOWLEDGE REQUIRED:

We need to fix the formatting information on the first track of the disk, then recreate the MBR. This is complicated on most RLL drives by the fact that information about the type of hard disk is larded in with format information on the first track of the disk. And each manufacturer uses a proprietary scheme that's not understood by others.

The MBR is located in the absolute top, outside track of the physical drive. It tells the computer what Operating System is active, what part of the disk it occupies, and where, precisely, more information can be found for booting that Operating System.

The MBR is created by FDISK, prior to DOS FORMAT. For disks prepared with FDISK and FORMAT under PC- or MS-DOS major Version 2.x, the MBR occupies the first sector, or 512 bytes, on the disk. The DOS boot record for the C: begins in the very next sector, typically followed by two copies of the File Allocation Table (FAT), the root directory, and then any files and subdirectories. If your disk was FOR-MATted under DOS 2, you're going to lose some data during recovery unless Mace or PC-Tools Deluxe were installed.

For disks FDISKed and FORMATted under DOS major Version 3.x, the MBR takes up the entire first track—usually 17 sectors. The DOS boot record, FATs, root directory and data begin on the next track, the one recorded on the bottom side of the top-most platter. If your disk was formatted under DOS 3 or higher, you'll have a slight chance of recovering 100 percent, but will likely lose some data unless Mace of PC-Tools Deluxe were installed.

Regardless of whose software you use, all low-level format programs format at least one whole track at a time, not single sectors. They replace any data recorded on the disk with a fill pattern. You can see, for disks formatted under DOS major Version 2, this poses a problem: to cure the first sector we must wipe-out sixteen sectors of vital information. With DOS major Version 3 we're in better shape; the MBR occupies the whole first track.

Knowledge Required

CURE: If you have a low-level format program from the manufacturer of the disk controller or hard disk on a card, you can attempt recovery. The recommended procedure at this point is to obtain the Htest/Hformat package listed in the back of the book and use GETSEC to save all the data on the first five cylinders of the disk. If you do this, you leave yourself with the best chance of 100 percent recovery, no matter what difficulties are encountered. If you don't use GETSEC, some data loss is inevitable, and any mistake you make beyond this point could be irreversible.

If your disk was formatted with DOS major Version 2.x, as I pointed out above, we have an immediate dilemma: the Master Boot Record occupies only one sector, the balance of the first track being devoted to DOS boot, FAT, and possible root directory information.

Cure

If you use GETSEC, note any reported errors. We already know there are errors on head 0, track 0, but make a note of any errors beyond that point. It may be necessary to low-level format those areas as well.

Using GETSEC, make a copy of the first five cylinders on the drive. Put the copy aside. It'll go a long way towards making 100 percent recovery possible as we're forced to use the manufacturer's format program.

Next, we need to do a low-level format of the corrupted track. This is not the same as a DOS FORMAT, which, on a hard disk is almost always "logical." This is a simple verification. Low-level formatters come either as a separate diagnostic disk, or third party software, such as Htest/Hformat, or built into some third-party hard disk controller cards.

To determine if your machine has a low-level format program built-in, you'll need a copy of DEBUG.COM or DEBUG.EXE in the A: drive. From the A> prompt:

Type DEBUG and press RETURN.

Type G = C800:5 and press RETURN.

If the format program appears, **do nothing!** Skip the next paragraph.

If nothing happens immediately, you don't have a built-in low-level formatter. You'll have to reboot your machine by pressing Ctrl-Alt-Del, or possibly by turning the power off and on. You'll need third party software, such as Htest/Hformat.

Cure

To recover an RLL type drive, you generally have no choice but to run the low-level formatter from the card manufacturer and immediately kill the power. That is, tell it to go ahead and the moment you hit RETURN, pull the plug, or hit the BIG RED SWITCH on the side or back of the machine. This should repair the defective track 0. It'll also clobber some good tracks, which is why we used GETSEC.

Low-level format completed? Run FDISK or XFDISK again, option 4, "View disk parameters". If you get an error instead—no point denying it—that's not good news. It means the format information didn't take.

We're looking for the "No partitions defined" message. That's our signal for initial success. If you can't get past the error message, you still have one good chance. Turn to the diagnostic titled Track 0 Low-Level Format Failed.

Our next step is to redefine the lost partition information in the Master Boot Record. The main menu of either DOS FDISK or Kolod's XFDISK contains an option titled "Define DOS partition." Select it. Most likely your C: drive started at cylinder 0 and you used the entire disk for DOS. If not, you'll have to supply the best guess.

Cure

With XFDISK there's no penalty for mistakes, other than time spent trying new combinations if the first guess doesn't work. When DOS FDISK runs it tries to verify that the vital areas of the disk are error free. In the process, it not only reconstructs a MBR, it also wipes out the FATs, root directory, and some data on the partition being defined. XFDISK doesn't; it merely recreates the MBR.

After XFDISK has defined the MBR, it prompts you to press a key to reboot. You'll still need a DOS system disk in A:. Press ESCape.

If you don't have XFDISK and GET-SEC, you're now at a stage equivalent to an accidental FORMAT of your disk. No matter what version of DOS was used to originally format the drive, we have wiped out some vital information while formatting track 0.

If Mace or PC-Tools Deluxe were installed, turn to the section of this book

Cure

on recovering from Unintentional FORMAT of a Hard Disk. You'll get a near-perfect recovery.

If Mace or PC-Tools Deluxe weren't installed, you can use either one to get a large portion of your data back, though not necessarily the one thing you wanted most.

Before you try anything else, you should first try using PUTSEC to replace everything you GETSECed, except the very first sector (for DOS 2 disks) or track (for DOS 3 disks). That is, we want to replace everything *except* the MBR. You just created a new, good one, and the copy made by GETSEC contains junk or nothing. It was bad when you made the copy. What lies beyond the MBR, however, is the DOS boot, FATs, and root directory. If you can successfully restore them with PUTSEC, you'll be able to reboot the machine and recover 100 percent without Mace or PC-Tools Deluxe.

After restoring with PUTSEC, the machine should reboot from C: as if nothing had ever happened. Run the DOS program CHKDSK. If it reports no error, congratulations! Now, make an immediate backup of all your data. At the very least, copy all your valuable files to diskette or to some other physical drive or Bernoulli cartridge. You may have suffered one-time failure due to unknown hardware, software, or environmental events. Then again, you may have a major problem lurking. Read the section of this book titled Staying Out of Trouble.

If the machine didn't reboot from C:, or CHKDSK reported errors, relax. Close the A: drive door, reboot the machine from the DOS floppy.

Let's review the possibilities:

The partition may be there, but still be marked "Not active". Run XFDISK or FDISK selection 4, "View partition information." The "Status" column should show "A" for "Active" next to the DOS partition. If it shows "N," then you'll need to select from the main menu the "Change active partition" option and make the DOS partition "Active." Open the A: drive door, press ESCape and the machine should reboot from C:. Run CHKDSK. If no errors are reported, backup immediately and read the section Staying Out of Trouble.

Track 0 may be too weak to hold format information. XFDISK appeared to work, but each time you reboot you're right back where you started. Got to the diagnostic titled Track 0 Low-Level Format Failed.

C: is there but CHKDSK reports errors. On a disk originally formatted with DOS major Version 2 we wiped out some vital information while formatting track 0. You should already have restored track 0 with companion program, PUTSEC. If not, do that now. Then run XFDISK again, define a partition, reboot, run

Cure

CHKDSK again, and all should be well.

CHKDSK or DOS persist in reporting errors. It's likely that the disk was screwed up beyond the first track. You probably noted these errors when you ran GETSEC. Reformatting track zero usually makes these errors go away. In this case, we weren't so lucky. But that's why we saved five cylinders of data at the outset, and noted the errors.

Cure

If your machine was opened for any reason just before all this trouble came upon it, or was moved, dropped, or had coffee spilled into its cooling slots, you should consider opening it now. Check all the cards. It wouldn't be a bad idea to pull them out and then put them back in. Check all the cables. I know, you didn't touch any cables, but check them anyway, both ends, where they connect to the card and to the disk.

It's possible that you have a bad disk controller card. If it's not out of the question, you might consider swapping controller cards with another machine, a friend, or your faithful local dealer. Because, from here on in 100 percent recovery is out the window.

If nothing else works, you'll have to low-level format all the tracks on all the heads that reported errors, from cylinder 0 to cylinder 4 (for a total of 5.) This is the area DOS uses for system information. You should PUTSEC again afterwards, XFDISK, and reboot.

Cure

Check for your most valuable files. Run CHKDSK, but don't be intimidated by errors. If you can copy off your most valuable files, do it now. Check their integrity. Some things are just not going to look right.

When you've got everything you can get at, stop and turn to the section on Recovering From Accidental FORMAT. Mace, and more recently PC-Tools Deluxe, have the power to reconstruct the DOS system areas from data elsewhere on the disk, which describes the situation you're in: good data, bad FATs and root directory.

SUMMARY:

You can start over from scratch, FDISKing and running DOS FORMAT. You can restore from backups, if you have them. If Mace, Norton Advanced, or PC-Tools Deluxe were installed, you can FDISK, then restore as if from an accidental FORMAT and get substantial recovery. Or you can get the Htest software and use its XFDISK utility to completely recover.

"Invalid Drive Specification" Message. Track 0 Low-Level Format Failed

DIAGNOSIS: Either your disk controller card is bad and must be replaced, or the disk is unusable and must be repaired, or there's something wrong with your computer that wants fixing. But you may still recover the data.

TOOLS REQUIRED: A second controller card of the same type. You may need a second good hard disk identical to the dead one, or at least with the same number of heads, and the GETSEC and PUTSEC programs from the Htest Hformat package listed in the back of the book. Compaq owners who don't already own one may want to get a Torqx #15 screwdriver from the local hardware store.

KNOWLEDGE REQUIRED: Without a good track 0, DOS will never use the disk again. That's where the Master Boot Record must go. There are no alternatives. Three things can cause track 0 to fail: a dud hard disk controller card, a dud hard disk, or a dud computer.

The most effective way of isolating the problem is swapping components with known good equipment: yours, a friend's, or your trusty local dealer's.

You can also test with something like Htest, for integrity of the hard disk controller and extent of the problem. It may be possible to read the data off the disk onto another or to floppies, and place it on a good hard disk for recovery. We have done this successfully many times, even on large, dedicated Novell file-servers. It's a simple but time-consuming process.

If the disk mechanism itself is physically damaged—a bad head, a bad stepper motor, voice-coil, or the thing just won't spin anymore—all is not completely lost, but recovery is going to involve finding and securing the cooperation of repair people or possibly the manufacturer.

At some point you'll have to decide whether it's worth the time, money, and effort to recover. It may be simpler to rekey the information, or chalk the whole thing up to experience. I'll try to keep you apprised at each stage of how far you've come and what's ahead.

Knowledge Required

QUICK CURE:

If you have a machine with an identical drive and you have at least once in your life opened a machine and wiggled a cable, or added in a card, try this: faking the machine into thinking the bad drive is the good one.

We're going to take advantage here of the fact that DOS only reads the Master Boot Record once, at power-up. Turn off the power. Remove the bad

Quick Cure

drive from its machine. This involves no more than disconnecting one or two cables and removing the screws that hold it in its slot. (On a Compaq, you may need a stubby screwdriver, as the drive is secured from the sides.)

Turn off the power and open the good machine. What we are going to do here is trick the machine into thinking the bad drive is the good one. This isn't a dangerous undertaking, but it doesn't always work.

First find a free power supply cable—not a ribbon cable, but a milk-white plastic connector with four colored wires. There'll be one entering the back of your existing hard disk and one entering the back of each floppy drive. You'll likely see one or two free ones. If not, don't worry, we'll take one off the floppy drive when the moment comes.

Position your bad drive where it's close to a power cable. On top of the power supply usually works. That's the chrome shield with all the holes in it. Just set it there for now. There's nothing mystical about where hard disks are standing while they work. If you have a free power connector, plug it into the hole in the back of the bad drive. It'll only fit one way. Now, turn on the machine. It'll boot from the good drive.

Wait until you get the C> prompt. If you don't have a free power cable, now is the time to remove the one connected to your floppy drive. There may be a lot of cables, so go slowly. Be patient. The

Quick Cure

power connectors are often stubborn. Wiggle and pull as best you can. It'll come out. When it does, plug it into the bad drive.

The next step is the tricky one. You have to wiggle the two ribbon cables (one on a Compaq) off the good hard disk and onto the bad disk. You'll see thin cables leaving the disk controller card, a relatively narrow 20 wire cable, and a wider 36 wire cable. The wider one may have a free connector on it. That's for your second hard disk. We want the one connected to your good drive C:. Wiggle it off. It fits around a tongue, like the one on the back of your bad drive. You may be working in cramped quarters with your fingers down in a bunch of wires and cables. That can't be helped. Be patient and wiggle; it will come off, and so will the narrow cable.

The cables are usually keyed—the connector fitted with a tooth and the tongue on the drive notched to accept it—so they only go on one way. You want to slide both cables onto the back of the bad drive.

Once connected, go to the keyboard, type DIR and press RETURN for a directory of C:. You should see a directory of your old, bad drive. Run the DOS program CHKDSK. It should report all is well.

If the machine appears to hang up, turn off the power. If you never tested the bad drive with a good controller, here's your chance. Turn the power on and see if you get a good boot-up. If

Quick Cure

that doesn't work, you have to power-down and replace the cables in their original positions. You can either try again or move on to Cure #2.

IF CHKDSK reports all is well, backup or copy your valuable files to floppies. (Remember, if you stole the floppy power supply, you'll have to find it a power cable, perhaps the one that's now powering your disconnected original C: drive.)

CURE #1:   You'll need Htest to do a low-level diagnostic of the dead drive. It'll tell you if the hard disk controller is bad, and if it is you'll need a replacement, preferably identical. If it's an RLL controller, an identical replacement is absolutely required. If the controller diagnoses bad, go to CURE #3.

If the controller passes its basic checks, Htest will go ahead and test for errors on the disk. If it reports that every head, track and sector is bad, you'll need to replace the controller. Again, an identical replacement is best. If it's an RLL controller, an identical replacement is absolutely required.

If Htest fails track 0 but reads the rest of the disk with few or no errors, you're in luck, provided you can come up with a good hard disk that's identical (for PCs or XTs), or that has the same or greater number of heads and equal or greater tracks or cylinders for AT-class machines. When you define drive type at setup on an AT, it will only use as many heads and tracks as the internal drive table specifies for that type. Thus, you can fake a smaller drive.

What you need to do is use GETSEC to dump all the tracks, except head 0, track 0 on the dead disk to floppies or to another drive. If you have a DOS major Version 2 formatted drive, you'll also need to capture sectors 2–17 on head 0, track 0. GETSEC will fill out unreadable areas with dummy data, providing us with as close to a mirror image of the data as possible. You can then use PUTSEC to place the data back on the good drive. I'll assume you either backed up the good drive, or bought a new one.

Cure #1

Once you GETSEC the data, remove the bad drive and put it to one side. Don't throw it away yet. PUTSEC is the mirror reverse of GETSEC; we can use it to restore the data from the bad drive to the good one, with the exception of the master boot record. The good drive already has a good Master Boot Record. Provided you weren't seeing extensive errors during GET-SEC, you should be able to reboot the machine with Ctrl-Alt-Del, or turn the power off and on, and it'll come up as before. Run the DOS program CHKDSK.

CURE #2:

We're going to open your machine and check all the connections here. I'll tell you what to do and what not to. If you really don't feel comfortable about

Cure #2

opening up your computer, get someone else to wield the screwdriver while you read the instructions. Or else skip this section and go to CURE #2, which involves Htest and is software only.

Ready? **Turn off the power! Unplug the computer!**

Let's make sure your existing controller card is properly connected and seated. You'll have to remove some screws (usually 5 from the back or 4 from the sides) and slide the lid off your computer. Compaq's have oddball Torx 15 screws; you'll want a Torx 15 screwdriver from your local hardware store. Most lids slide forward, Zenith's mostly slide back. The manual for the machine usually shows a diagram under the heading for memory expansion.

Inside there'll be at least one printed circuit board with one (Compaq) or two flat blue-gray ribbon cables connecting it to the hard disk.

Note: one edge of each cable is colored, usually blue or red. This signifies **pin 1** on the cables. The colored edges should all be oriented the same way: all up, all down, all left, or all right. It's consistency that counts. If they're not, and the machine was recently opened for service or some other reason and came back dead, odds are a cable got put back the wrong way.

If you have more than two cables, make the odd one out agree with the others. If you have one cable and a Compaq, fear not. It only fits one way. If you're not certain which of the two is correct, you'll have to get out your

Cure #2

magnifying glass and look at the board. There may be a tiny "1" printed next to pin 1, or one of the posts the cable attaches to may be square, or the plastic part attached to the board may have a mitered corner.

You'll probably have to feel for the ends of the cables where they connect to the drive. The power is OFF—right? Look as best you can and feel that the end are pressed tightly onto the drive and, again, the cables oriented with the stripes on the same side.

Now, place a thumb on the back and front edge of the controller board and rock it front to back while slowly applying more and more downward pressure. What we're doing here is making sure there's complete contact between the board and the connector it fits into. Stop, and make sure the board is level.

Look at the ends of the ribbon cables; they should be fully seated on the board, no gaps or gold pins visible between the plastic end of the cable and the plastic connector on the board. If gaps show, or the two pieces come together cockeyed, you'll want to squeeze them together. You may have to pry them apart first. Note the colored edge on the cable before taking apart any connection. Make certain the colored edge gets put back on in the same orientation.

Now, turn the power ON! Yes, the lid is still open. Keep your fingers out, unless you know what you're doing. It's not all that dangerous, but it's not necessary to probe.

Cure #2

Listen. Did the hard disk whine when the power came up? If you didn't notice, power off and listen for the disk winding down. Power on again. You should hear the hard disk coming up to speed. If not, it's either dead or the power is disconnected.

If the machine booted from C:, congratulations! Turn off the power, close the lid, screw it on, then power-up and backup your data, or at least copy the valuable stuff to some other place.

CURE #3: We're going to swap controller cards. I'll assume you've tried CURE #2 and gotten nowhere.

If you have an RLL controller, one that packs 50 percent or more extra data into the same space as an ordinary controller, *you must have an identical replacement*. If you have an MFM controller, or don't know, you ought to have an identical replacement, but some other controller may work.

Note the orientation of the colored edge of the ribbon cables; they'll go the same way on the new controller card.

Power off! My concern isn't for you so much as for your machine. Much more likely you would hurt it by dropping a screw and shorting out a chip, than it would hurt you, so long as you *never, ever open the chrome cage that surrounds the power supply*.

Remove the retaining screw in the chrome bracket at the back of the disk controller card. Try not to drop it at the last minute into the machine. (If you do drop it, don't waste time with your fingers. Get some cellophane tape and use your screwdriver and fingers to maneuver one end of the tape onto the screw. Don't use a magnet.)

Disconnect the cables from the drive controller card. You may need a screwdriver or knife to get the connectors to start separating, but just to start them. Get a little gap, then use your fingers. Wiggle and pry. Be patient; they'll come apart.

Same when pulling the card. Rock it forward and back, pulling upwards. You can pry under the chrome bracket a little, but don't get one end way up in the air and the other cocked down, or you'll get nowhere. Be patient, be determined, and it will come out.

Cure #3

The new card goes in the same way, only you are pressing down, rocking fore and aft. How much pressure? A good rule would be your heels should never leave the ground.

If the back end stops with maybe a quarter-inch gap between the chrome lip and the body of the computer, hold on a minute. The bottom of the card bracket is probably hung up, either on the chassis or the back edge of the main printed circuit board. Look down where the bracket slides along the inside back of the chassis. You may need a finger on the back outside to wiggle it some and get it to slide down.

The bracket should come firmly to rest on the chassis where the screw holds, with the card level in its slot. If not, pull the card and try again.

Cure #3

Once the card is in, reconnect the cables with the same orientation as before. If you have a different card, you may have to change the orientation.

All connected? Power on. The machine will try to boot. If you get to the C> prompt, and DOS CHKDSK reports all's well, congratulations. Backup your data right now. If the boot fails, read on.

CURE #4:   We know it's not the controller, or the cables. We know it's not the machine. We know it's the drive. All's not lost, but unless you're adventurous or technically inclined, you're going to need some professional help beyond this point.

Many of the common drives, especially Seagates, have a printed circuit board attached to the bottom of the drive. This board can be swapped with one from an identical good drive, either by you, by a dealer technician, or a drive repair shop.

Insist on being present. You don't want them to do any testing or formatting that might be destructive. They may insist to you that all's lost anyway. Pay no attention to them. If necessary, pick up the drive, pay the bill, and leave. It's best to describe what you want them to do as best you can beforehand.

If your diagnostic software consistently reported errors on one head, while all other heads reported good, your last hope is to have a drive repair

Cure #4

shop open the drive, remove the platters, and place them in the body of a good drive. It's possible in many drives to read disks removed from another of the same type, provided they haven't been physically destroyed by grinding heads.

Don't open the drive yourself. The inside of a hard disk is clean, dirt and dust-free. From the perspective of a hard disk head flying low over the platter, even a human hair is the size of a log. Also, a running, open hard disk is a dangerous thing. It can shed parts. Secure the cooperation of a drive repair shop.

SUMMARY:

So long as the physical platters aren't damaged, there is hope for recovery. This may involve opening the machine and checking or replacing the cables or controller card, or the drive itself. It may involve careful repair of the drive, or dumping the data with GETSEC, then PUTSECing it onto another drive. Success is possible, though it might be less stressful for those of you who don't feel comfortable mucking around inside your computer to simply accept the loss and key it all back in.

Glossary

ASCII American Standard Code for Information Interchange. Refers to a standard set of 128 alphabetic, numeric, punctuation and control characters. Additional foreign and graphics characters on your PC are not part of the standard ASCII set.

Attribute byte See file attribute.

AUTOEXEC.BAT An optional batch file that automatically executes every time the computer is turned on or rebooted. Typically it sets the PATH and PROMPT and other items in the system, according to your preferences.

bad sector An area of the disk that will no longer reliably record data.

Bernoulli Box Removable media drive manufactured by Iomega Corp.

BIOS Basic Input Output System. The code built into the machine that effects the transfer of data to and from disks, printers, keyboards, mice, the screen, and other devices.

Boot Record The very first sector of each DOS partition on the disk or diskette, it contains information about the partition and a small, executable program that loads DOS and starts it running.

CHKDSK A DOS program that checks the disk or diskette for file structure errors.

cluster A unit of storage comprised of one or more sectors. DOS always allocates space to a file a cluster at a time, even if the file consists of a single character.

COMMAND.COM The portion of DOS that accepts your typed commands and translates them into actions, such as providing a directory listing when you type DIR, or executing a program when you type its name.

CONFIG.SYS An optional list of configuration commands processed every time the machine is turned on or rebooted. Typically it lists the number of files that can be open at one time, as well as device drivers, such as ramdisks, disk caching programs, or the ANSI screen driver.

controller card The card in your computer that controls the flow of data to and from the hard disk or floppy disk

crash Sudden dramatic failure of a disk. Sometimes this is actually the result of a head striking a platter.

CRC See Cyclic Redundancy Check.

cross-linked files The File Allocation Table for two different files points to the the same space on the disk. That's not allowed. All files, even duplicates, are stored in separate areas.

Cyclic Redundancy Check When data are written to disk, the coded values for each character are multiplied according to a standard formula and the resulting number is stored at the end of each sector. Subsequent reads repeat the multiplication and the resulting number is compared to the original. If they don't match, an "error reading data" message is displayed.

cylinder Data are stored in concentric rings, called tracks, from top to bottom on each recording surface or platter. Each stack of rings is numbered from zero, beginning at the outer edge, and is known collectively as a cylinder.

cylinder 0 The outermost stack of data tracks where the Master Boot Record is stored.

device driver A program loaded by CONFIG.SYS, which interfaces your computer to some storage device, such as a disk, or other input and output devices, such as printers, plotters, keyboards, and mice.

direct memory access Hardware built into your computer that allows data to move to and from memory without interrupting the central processor.

DMA See Direct Memory Access.

DOS Disk Operating System. Three programs that load, execute, and mediate between your application and your computer. These are the "system files" IBMBIO.COM and IBMDOS.COM, which are hidden, and COM-MAND.COM. Under some versions of MS-DOS, the first two files are called IO.SYS and MSDOS.COM. There is no functional difference between PC-DOS and MS-DOS, but there are subtle differences introduced by IBM, Microsoft, and various computer manufucturers that can cause problems if you mix them up or change versions.

Enhanced Small Device Interface A modern standard that defines the way data can be transferred to and from intelligent devices such as disks. Requires new hardware, but offers higher performance.

ESDI See Enhanced Small Device Interface.

Extended Partition Under DOS Versions 3.0 and later, large capacity disks can be divided into a primary bootable partition called C:, and an extended partition, which may be divided into one or more logical drives, each with its own letter.

FAT See File Allocation Table.

FDISK The DOS utility program used to define (or remove) a logical DOS partition, known usually as C:, on a physical disk. Under DOS Version 3.0 and later, an extended partition and other drive letters may also be assigned.

File Allocation Table The FAT. A map corresponding to available storage space on a DOS disk or diskette. When a file is written to disk, the corresponing area in the FAT is marked.

file attribute The character right after the extension in a file's directory entry, which can be set to reflect certain qualities, such as "Read-only," "Hidden," or "System."

FORMAT.COM A DOS utility program that checks the disk for errors, then intializes the boot record, FAT and root directory areas in preparation for data storage.

head The electromagnetic recording head that reads and writes data to the disk.

head parking Moving the recording head to an area where no data are stored to prevent an accidental "head crash" if the computer is moved.

hexadecimal number A base 16 number. We're accustomed to thinking decimally: what comes after 9 is 10. Programmers and computers work in powers of 2—4,8,16. In hexadecimal (hex) notation, what comes after 9 is A, then B,C,D,E,F. Then comes 10, which is really 17 decimal. Got that?

hidden file A file whose "hidden" attribute is marked. You won't see it when you do a DIR, but it's visible to DOS.

high-level formatting Logical information prepared by programs, such as DOS FORMAT.COM, on a disk that has already been marked with low-level recording information and partitioned with FDISK for use as a DOS partition.

IBMBIO.COM An essential DOS system file. It corrects and extends the computer's built-in BIOS functions.

IBMDOS.COM An essential DOS system file.

IO.SYS The MS-DOS equivalent of IBMBIO.COM.

interleave Refers to the sequence in which sectors are recorded on a track. Each sector carries with it a number, typically 1 through 17. They do not have to come in numeric sequence, and usually do not. At low-level format time the sequence can be set to give the computer a breather between sectors 1 and 2, time to process the data from sector one before 2 passes under the recording head.

interrupt Programs interract with the computer hardware by "interrupting" the normal execution of code with instructions to the machine. In interrupt is an instruction to the computer to stop what it was doing and execute some hardware-specific instructions, then return to its previous activity.

kilobyte 1024 bytes or characters.

logical drive Storage space collectively assigned to a drive letter, such as

C:. It may be all, or only part of a physical disk. On some systems it may not be a disk at all, but a chunk of RAM or a tape drive that looks to DOS (and you) as if it were.

low-level formatting The process of testing and recording information on a blank hard disk, most often performed by dealers or distributors. This is where interleave is determined.

Master Boot Record The very first physical sectors on the top, outermost track on a hard disk. It holds information about the size and low-level format of the disk, and what operating system(s) occupy what areas. This is where FDISK records partition information. It must be remain defect-free for the disk to be usable.

Mean Time Between Failures The number of hours at which half of all drives of a certain type will have failed. This is a statistical evaluation. It means one in two drives will be dead after that many hours service. Yours may run twice as long; then again, it may die the day you turn on the machine. The important thing is, the higher the MTBF, the more rugged the drive, assuming always that the figure is honest and based on experience, not an engineer's best guess.

medium The stuff on which the data is recorded, usually iron oxide (rust) or thin-plated magnetic film. Loosely, this means the plastic or metal disk that holds the medium as well.

memory resident program A program that remains in memory after returning you to DOS. Under some condition, a certain special keystroke or timed delay, the resident program usurps control. The important thing is, even though you are not directly aware of its presence, the resident program affects what happens on your machine, not always in a positive way.

MFM See Modified Frequency Modulation encoding.

Modified Frequency Modulation encoding The most commonly used encoding sheme for translating data into a signal that can be recorded on a disk.

MS-DOS See DOS.

MTBF See Mean Time Between Failures

orphaned clusters Space allocated in the FAT and the data stored in the corresponding areas of the disk have no directory entry.

parent directory The directory from which the current directory branches.

partition One or more cylinders on a physical disk assigned in the Master Boot Record to a particular operating system or drive letter.

PC-DOS See DOS.

physical drive The mechanism itself, seen as a whole, as opposed to the DOS logical devices known as C:, D:, etc.

plated media More expensive and durable thin-film coated disks, as opposed to oxide coated disks.

platter The (usually) metal disk that carries the recording medium.

power supply The transformer inside the computer that converts house current into power acceptable to the chips and printed circuits. It looks like a perforated chrome cage, and usually carries all sorts of warning stickers. Heed them.

proprietary format Some hard disk controllers use a special low-level format to prepare the disk. This is peculiar to the card's manufacturter and often to a particular model controller. That means you cannot later connect the drive to a different card and expect to read the data.

read-only file A file whose directory "read-only" attribute is marked "on". The file is write-protected; you cannot alter it or overwrite it.

read/write head The little electromagnet that actually emits the coded data impulses as it flys over the recording surface.

RECOVER A DOS utility that is both useless and dangerous. Don't even experiment with it.

RLL See Run Length Limited encoding.

ROM BIOS See BIOS.

root directory The primary directory from which all other directories branch. This is the one directory that is always in the same size and place on the disk, directly after the boot and FAT entries.

Run-Length Limited encoding A recently embraced scheme for recording data on hard disks that packs 50-100 percent more data in the same space.

SCSI See Small Computer Systems Interface.

sector A portion of a track, created by the low-level format. The smallest unit, usually 512 bytes, in which data can be stored on a physical disk.

Small Computer Systems Interface SCSI (scuzzy), is a new standard that defines how data are transferred to and from a computer, usually to a disk.

ST 506/412 The most common standard interface for disks and computers. It simply defines which electrical signals appear where on the connectors used to attach the disk to the computer, and what they mean.

starting cluster The part of a directory entry that says where in the FAT the file begins. Where the file goes from there on the disk is recorded in the FAT.

subdirectory A directory that branches from the root or from some other directory.

surge protector An inexpensive electrical device that stops high-voltage surges from traveling from your wall socket up the power cord into your computer or peripherals and likely fry thousands of dollars worth of delicate chips.

SYS.COM The MS-DOS equivalent of IBMDOS.COM.

system files See DOS.

track One of many concentric rings on a disk or diskette in which data are stored.

UnDELETE Reverses the effects of the DOS command DEL.

UnERASE Same as UnDELETE. It reverses the effect of the DOS command ERASE (which is the same as DEL).

UnFORMAT Reverses the effects of the DOS utility FORMAT.

uninterruptable power supply A battery that takes over when house current fails, preventing loss of data.

UPS See Uninterruptable Power Supply.

UPS software Programs that preserve the volatile contents of memory on disk and can restore the machine to a previous state in the event of a power outage or, more importantly, a forced reboot when a program locks-up the machine.

Appendix

Product Manufacturers

Bernoulli Box: removable media hard disks

Iomega Corporation
1821 West 400
South Ray, UT 84067
(408) 436-4922

dSALVAGE: dBASE file repair and recovery

Comtech Publishing
Box 456
Pittsford, NY 14534
(716) 586-3365

Fastback: floppy backup software

Fifth Generation Systems
11200 Industriplex Blvd.
Baton Rouge, LA 70809
(714) 553-0111

HardCard: reliable hard disk on a card

Plus Development
1778 McCarthy Blvd.
Milpitas, CA 95035
(408) 946-3700

HTEST: advanced hard disk diagnostic software

Paul Mace Software
400 Williamson Way
Ashland, OR 97520
(800) 523-0258

Mace Utilities 5.0 and Mace Gold: diagnostic, data recovery, dBASE and word processing file repair, protection and speedup software.

Paul Mace Software
400 Williamson Way
Ashland, OR 97520
(800) 523-0258

Maynard Maynstream: streaming tape backup

Maynard Electronics
460 E. Semoran Blvd.
Casselberry, FL 32707
(305) 331-6402

Memory Minder: Floppy drive diagnostic software.

J&M Systems
15100-A Central S.E.
Albuquerque, NM 87123
(505) 292-4182

Miniscribe: economical hard disks

Miniscribe Corporation
1861 Lefthand Circle
Longmont, CO 80501
(303) 651-6000

Newbury: high capacity hard disks

Newbury Data Incorporated
9800 North Lamar Blvd. M/S 300
Austin, TX 78753
(512) 834-7746

Norton Utilities: diagnostic, data recovery, and speedup software

Peter Norton Computing
2210 Wilshire Blvd. #186
Santa Monica, CA 90403
(213) 453-2361

PC-Tools: diagnostic, data recovery, and speedup software

Central Point Software
15220 N.W. Greenbriar Pkwy. #200
Beaverton, OR 97006
(503) 690-8090

Rescue: Lotus 1-2-3 file recovery and repair

Spectrum Computer Services
9 Burditt Rd.
North Reading, MA 01864
(800) 541-4370

Index

About the Author

Paul Mace was born and raised in the Finger Lakes district of upstate New York. He served four years in the United States Marine Corps navigating transport aircraft, including two years in Vietnam. He is a graduate of San Francisco State University with a degree in English and creative writing. Author of Mace Utilities and CEO of Mace Software, he currently lives in southern Oregon with his wife, Kathleen and two children.